A Simple Seller

OF NOODLES

DR. CB SKELTON

a Simple Seller
OF NOODLES

a memoir

TATE PUBLISHING
AND ENTERPRISES, LLC

Published by Tate Publishing & Enterprises, LLC
127 E. Trade Center Terrace | Mustang, Oklahoma 73064 USA
1.888.361.9473 | www.tatepublishing.com

Tate Publishing is committed to excellence in the publishing industry. The company reflects the philosophy established by the founders, based on Psalm 68:11, *"The Lord gave the word and great was the company of those who published it."*

Book design copyright © 2011 by Tate Publishing, LLC. All rights reserved.
Cover design by Kenna Davis
Interior design by Nathan Harmony

Published in the United States of America

ISBN: 978-1-61346-719-0
1. Biography & Autobiography / Military
2. Biography & Autobiography / Personal Memoirs
11.10.03

A NOTE FROM THE AUTHOR

Although it was a story that needed to be told, when the incredible nature of SamSan Ouch's life saga first became obvious to me, no thought of my writing a book crossed my mind. A friend of mine made statements on many occasions that he planned to put the story into a book form. More than twenty years passed, and pen had not been put to paper, so it became my duty to share the story of lifelong protection and provision for an imperfect Christian in many seemingly impossible situations.

My only previous writing experience had been with scientific papers or poetry. Therefore, even at my advanced age, I took a couple of computer writing courses to prepare myself for the task.

For several years, SamSan was unwilling to share many of his life details for fear that harm would come to some of his relatives who remained in Cambodia. By the time the mantle had fallen on me, SamSan had become totally deaf as a result of one of his near-death experiences when he stood close to an ammunition dump that exploded when it was struck by a Khmer Rouge rocket. This made the task of garnering details much more time consuming and difficult. Because of his deafness, all interviews had to be conducted with questions written on paper, followed by a verbal response.

SamSan is the sole source of all information in this book that occurred prior to his arrival in the United States, with the exception of one short episode related by two other members of our refugee family.

No attempt is made by either the author or the main character of the book to hide the human flaws of its main character. As Flip Wilson used to say, "What you see is what you get." At SamSan's insistence, names of persons and places have not been changed, and verbal consent has been obtained wherever possible.

The author hopes that by seeing the evidence of a protective hand repeatedly placed on a modern-day Christian who has many imperfections, the reader will not only be entertained but will be encouraged in his or her walk.

—CBS

PROLOGUE

"If he is still alive, my oldest son would be about six years old now, and he must surely think I have deserted him," said SamSan Ouch in one of our earliest conversations. He sat wide-eyed and stiffly erect as he continued, "Nothing could be farther from the truth. I have made every effort to find him, and I shall never give up my search until I either find my son or know for certain what happened to him. I understand how he must feel, because history does tend to repeat itself, and my natural parents deserted me early in life."

He managed a slight smile. "There have been quite a number of strange stories about people who had been lost in the awful confusion of the Khmer Rouge regime and then resurfaced a long time later. That is why we still hold on to a small ray of hope for the boy even after this length of time."

SamSan's woeful words ushered me into a world I had wanted to believe existed only in fiction. But the tone of voice rang true in this leader of a group of ten Cambodians who had come to the United States in 1980 from the Kaoidang Refugee Holding Center in Thailand. My church—the First Baptist Church of Winder, Georgia—had agreed to serve as the sponsor for them.

When I pressed the young Cambodian to give me more details about his son, he responded, "I wish I felt free to tell you my entire story. I honestly believe it is stranger and more dramatic than anything you might have seen in the movie, *The Killing Fields*. However, I still have kinfolk in Cambodia who might face great danger even at this late date if certain details of the story got back to certain people in that country."

SamSan's scintillating story, gleaned through a series of many casual conversations and a large number of formal and informal interviews over a period of more than twenty-five years, can now be safely told.

Raison d'Etre in Winder, Georgia

Winder, Georgia—October 1979

How SamSan and his fellow refugees came to live in the small town of Winder, Georgia, is an intriguing story in itself. Nothing that compared to that group's coming to the area had ever happened in our small town before the First Baptist Church held a missions conference in the early fall of 1979. Rev. Jerry Baker from the Georgia Baptist Convention headquarters loudly exhorted his audience at the conference as he said:

"You see the pictures of those pitiful, starving babies from Southeast Asia with their huge, swollen bellies on TV every night, and it breaks your hearts. Those children and their equally pitiful, starving parents need more than your money and your prayers. They need homes." He paused briefly for emphasis before he added, "And they need Jesus Christ.

"For several years, they have stared death in the face daily—death by starvation or death at the hands of cruel dictators. If they remained in their homelands, it meant a certain future of death or a hopeless life under communist dictatorship. Therefore, they escaped—many of them through a hail of bullets—hoping to find a better life for themselves and their families. Now, they are facing something every day that is almost as terrible as death. They live in horrible conditions, in squalid refugee camps where raw sewage constantly runs through open ditches and most of their streets. They have little or no hope unless we give that hope to them."

His words struck home. Shaken to its core, our sedate small church felt it must take some type of action to help these pitiful people. The missions committee of the church appointed a subcommittee to sponsor a refugee family, and they named me as its chairman.

Why me? I thought. I had a wife, six children to look after, and a busy medical practice to run. It had taken me nearly thirty years to build up that following. There were babies to deliver and broken arms to set—and there were my duties as chairman of deacons in the church. How could I take on the responsibility for an added family—a foreign family at that?

On the other hand, I had been the person who made the motion that we become a refugee family sponsor. I should have known better.

Preparations

The committee immediately secured a wooden-clapboard house of early-1900's vintage, located diagonally across from the rear of the church campus. We jumped quickly through the required paperwork hoops for sponsoring a refugee family. Eager volunteers went to work using donated materials to remodel the old house; would-be carpenters sawed and hammered at floors, walls, and ceilings. Pretend plumbers made needed repairs to the ancient pipes and fixtures in the house. Elementary electricians elected to make little change to the status quo of the house's wiring. With so much volunteer help, we soon had the ancient house a bit closer to the 1979 local standard housing code.

Volunteer painters as young as six brightened up the repaired plaster walls inside the house by daubing donated paint on them. The exterior walls had served very well in their unpainted condition for their nearly eighty-year lifespan; therefore, the committee elected to leave them unpainted.

Nevermind the fact that the old house had only one bathroom. The chances were good that any Southeast Asian refugee who might come to live in the house had never lived in its equal, even in its unpainted state and with its sparse bath facilities.

Fashion? Given no thought in preparing the place. Function and cost had to be the only considerations. The committee furnished the house with a collage of old furniture donated by church members. When we had collected a considerable quantity of used clothing, curtains, and other donated soft goods, we stored them along with a few staple groceries. Now we felt ready and eager for action.

We waited impatiently while the Georgia Baptist Convention negotiated with the State Department about a family from Laos—a disabled man, his wife, and ten children. Information from the Convention said no one in the household spoke English. To compound the problem, we had no assurance that anyone in the family would be able to work and help us in providing support for them. We shuddered at the thought of taking on such a difficult family, but we felt that God had truly called our church to become a sponsor. Consequently, we reluctantly agreed to accept them. On three different occasions, we expected their arrival, only to learn of its cancellation.

On the third occasion, the State Department stood firm in its refusal to admit the family to the United States. The committee breathed a collective sigh of relief, but the debacle had put us at least three months behind our projected schedule. It meant that any children in whatever family we might sponsor would face the difficulty of entering school in the middle of the academic year.

Three additional months passed without a word from the Convention. I finally called Rev. Baker and said to him, "You have sold us on the pressing need for churches to sponsor refugee families. We have been ready and waiting for our family for the bigger part of a year. What is the problem now?"

"Oh, Doc," he said, "I am sorry. Someone in this office laid your application aside after the fiasco with the Laotian family, but you will get the next available family. While we have been on the phone, I have already moved Winder First Baptist to the head of the list on our computer. Please forgive us and be patient a while longer. It should not be long before you get some action."

A few days later, an anonymous caller from the Convention said, "We have a Cambodian family of ten already on the ground in California, and they have no assigned place to go. Their original sponsor has encountered a problem and cannot take them at this time. Could you possibly take care of them right away?"

"Does anyone in the group speak English?" I asked.

"I don't know."

"How many adults are in the group?"

"I think there are five in this group, and I understand all of them are able to work," she added.

"It sounds like our real family is finally here," I replied with a grin. "Send 'em on right away."

Many questions flitted through my mind as my foot pressed heavily on the gas pedal of the church van, speeding toward the Atlanta airport the following day. Because we had received such a short advance notice of their arrival, we had been unable to locate a Cambodian interpreter for this first meeting with the family.

How will we communicate? How will our church and our community react to and relate with people from a Buddhist country? Why in the world did God ever call our church to do such a drastic and foolish thing?

Introductions

Atlanta International Airport—October 9, 1980

As they walked up the ramp in the Atlanta Airport, my party of ten Southeast Asians proved quite easy to spot. According to the paper given me from the Catholic Relief Association (the organization that paid the group's airfare to America), their leader went by the name of "Ouch, SamSan." When SamSan spotted the sign bearing his name that I held aloft, he pointed to it and broke into a broad smile. Then, like a good shepherd, he herded the group in my direction.

As the group came down the gangway, I sized SamSan up quickly: *Thirtyish; skin light in color for a Cambodian—possibly Chinese in origin; slightly receding black hair; eyes not typically Asian; probably 5'6"; shuffling gait, and obviously bone weary from travel.*

When they came through the gate, I extended my hand to greet SamSan and said, "Welcome to America and to the state of Georgia."

He forced a weary smile and bowed deeply as he grasped my hand gently in both of his. Suddenly, his face brightened and his smile became huge and vibrant. Before I could speak another word, he said, "Oh, Gedeon, Gedeon."

The fact that he had recognized the small metallic Gideon emblem I always wear on the lapel of my suit coat shocked me. I knew from reading Gideon literature that we only had sixteen Gideon members in the entire country of Cambodia when it fell to the Khmer Rouge. We had mourned the deaths of every one of those brave and dedicated men during the Pol Pot regime, so one would expect his exposure to the Gideons to have been very limited.

With all the nonchalance I could muster, I asked him, "How do you know about the Gideons?"

"My father and my mother were Gedeons," his answer came in a soft, almost reverent, tone.

Although he had difficulty in pronouncing the soft *I* sound in "Gideons," the grammar of his English response was perfect. That one spoken sentence provided the answer to my question about the Gideons as well as to my prayer about how we would communicate.

Introductions of the rest of the group occurred rather hurriedly: David, SamSan's infant son, only nineteen months old, was proudly presented first. Next came Muoy Keng, SamSan's wife, about thirty and six months pregnant. Then he introduced Tang, said to be

SamSan's sister-in-law, and her husband, Pong, both thirtyish. Pong and Tang were guardians for Ren, Tang's niece, about twelve, and Kang, Pong's nephew, who was about ten. Both children had lost their parents during the Khmer Rouge regime. Then came Lan, Tang's fortyish aunt, and her son, Samsien, nearly twenty-one, and his sister, Heav, about twelve years old.

I reveled in the overall picture; our family had finally arrived. SamSan spoke near perfect English and had a Christian background. There were six adults instead of five, and every one of them appeared to be able to work. That should be enough workers to make our family self-sufficient.

Our family, indeed, I mused. *Thank You, God. You only used that Laotian family to test our sincerity about being sponsors, and then You did not send them. Now You have sent us what looks like a real winner. Thank You,* I prayed quietly.

We wasted no time in airport conversation. Small talk needed to wait for another time and place. In America, we had schedules to meet, and those schedules called for us to hurry. We had to load their meager baggage into the church van and scoot to Winder. The church waited for us anxiously, and they had cooked supper. They were eager to meet our new charges, and the food might get cold. Moreover, we still had to help them set up housekeeping.

FORMATIVE YEARS
SamSan's Story Begins to Unfold

Winder, Georgia—Early November 1980

A few days after our refugee family arrived in Winder, I slipped away from my office a few minutes early to see how the group was faring. November had stolen a page from March's calendar, and a frigid front had moved into Georgia much earlier than is usual. That front brought beautiful, blue, cloudless skies, but it also brought cold, blustery, northeast winds and sub-freezing temperatures.

On my arrival at the house, the redolence of garlic, hot peppers, and some oriental spices my nose did not recognize filled my nostrils. All of the women were gathered in the kitchen cooking dinner. As soon as the men saw me, they dropped their work of chinking every small crack around each window and door with pieces of paper or small strips of rags. Their complaints about the cold weather were as profuse and sincere as their greetings.

"It seems so very cold to us," SamSan explained. "In Cambodia the temperature hardly ever gets below fifty degrees on the Fahrenheit scale."

"It is pretty cold," I answered, "and there is no insulation in this house because it was built many years before insulation became a standard feature in houses in the South. However, I must admit our committee did not think about insulation when we worked on the house. On the other hand, Widow Cox raised her family here, and she and all of her children seem to have fared pretty well."

When he and I huddled around a radiant gas heater to talk, SamSan insisted that the other men return to their work.

"SamSan," I said, "when we first met, you told me you began life as an orphan. Ever since I heard that, I have been as curious as a cat to know how that happened. However, you indicated that some member or members of your family still in Cambodia might be hurt if certain parts of your story got back to certain people there. Well, I have been thinking about that situation, and it dawned on me that you are thirty-five years old now. Surely none of your people could be hurt if you told me about something that happened thirty-five years ago—and I am about to die of sheer curiosity."

SamSan's brow furrowed as he said, "The one I am most worried about is my lost son, but it is probable that he is already dead. Even if he is still alive, I do not really believe it could hurt him if that part of my story got back to Cambodia."

"Do not increase anybody's danger," I insisted, "but I wish you would tell me whatever you can, just to satisfy my morbid curiosity."

SamSan's slightly crooked and yellowed teeth revealed themselves in his broad, knowing smile. *His teeth seem in amazingly good shape, considering the hell he has endured over the past several years,* I thought as he began his tale.

"All I know about the very earliest part of my life," he said, "is what my adoptive mother told me, plus what little more I learned on the one chance I had to visit my natural mother."

"When I was very small, my adoptive parents never breathed a word about how I came to be a part of their family, and for several years I had no reason to think it happened by any means other than by natural birth. However, when I learned my older brother, Chong Ky, had been adopted, I started to wonder about certain things, but my mother and father never volunteered a single fact—and I did not dare to ask.

"I suppose I really had no great desire to know at the time, or it might have been because I had such great respect for my parents and I did not want to appear not trust them. I really have no idea as to the reason why, but I failed to ask.

"Later on, when I was about eight or nine years old, the strangest thing happened: A couple I had never seen before came to our home one day. Mother made me hide behind a curtain in the adjoining bedroom's closet while she talked to them in the parlor. She threatened to spank me if I dared to move or make a single sound or show myself while the couple was there. That seemed very strange to me, because Mother had never threatened me before, and she usually wanted to show me off to everyone who came—but this time, she dared me to show myself.

"I could hear them talking in the next room, and it sounded as if they were speaking about me. That really aroused my curiosity, so I took a peek through the opening in the curtain. I could see the visiting woman's face fairly well, but I am sure she never saw me. I thought she was beautiful. I never could get a good look at her husband. The woman did almost all of the talking and, from what I heard her say, I felt certain she had to be my natural mother.

"I heard her ask Mother, 'How much would it take for us to get him back? We have some money now and we can afford to take care of him.'

"Mother answered her in her most resolute voice, 'No amount of money could ever buy him back. He is not for sale like an ox or a horse,' she almost shouted.

"When the couple finally went away, I asked Mother, 'Who was that woman? The way she spoke, it sounded as if she might be my birth mother.'

"Then Mother motioned for me to sit on a stool beside her chair. 'Before I answer your question,' she said, 'let me tell you a story. Then I will tell you how God brought you into our family.'

"'Is it a true story, or did you read it in a book?' I asked.

"'It is a true story,' she answered me ever so gently, 'and it started in 1944.'

"'That was before I was born,' I said.

"Mother replied, 'Yes, I know, and you cannot imagine the difference between Cambodia in 1944 and Cambodia as it is today. The whole world was at war and a small puppet group of Cambodian traitors controlled by the Vichy French theoretically ran our government. Actually, the Japanese had a large garrison of troops here, and those troops controlled the country. Everything and everyone obeyed the bidding of the Japanese soldiers. It was a truly perilous time, and we had very little freedom.'

"Did they hurt either you or my father?' I asked.

"'No, they did not hurt us, Son, but let me get on with my story.' She seemed a bit irritated by my interruption."

SamSan's adoptive mother's Story

Battambang, Cambodia—Summer of 1944

During those treacherous days of Japanese occupation, a teen-age peasant-girl named Hong Diep lived in Battambang with her Vietnamese family. Her Vietnamese name means "beautiful flower," and she lived up to the meaning of her name. She was gorgeous. Hong Diep was madly in love with another teenage Vietnamese peasant named Saing Dinh.

The couple planned to be married as soon as Saing Dinh could finish raising the money Hong Diep's father demanded as dowry for his daughter. However, money did not come easy for him or for a majority of the Vietnamese nationals who lived in Cambodia at the time and were considered lower-class citizens.

One day in late 1944, the couple sauntered along Road One toward the middle of town just before sunset. They admired the floating bamboo homes that lined the banks of the Sangker River and talked about owning one of their own some day. Near the place where the iron bridge that leads to Wat Kandal (a Buddhist temple) crosses the Sangker River, they stopped to watch the sunset and talk about their upcoming marriage. "Honestly, Saing Dinh," said Hong Diep, "a few months ago when the Japanese came here, I thought our plans might have to be changed. Now, I really cannot tell any difference in our lives except for the fact that I see Japanese soldiers everywhere and there are so many more checkpoints than we ever had before they came."

Saing Dinh laughed and said, "There is a reason why we do not notice any difference. Soldiers cannot take things away from a person who has nothing to begin with. The only people they have really bothered are the rich folks. If it takes riches for them to bother somebody, it is not likely they will ever bother us."

"Oh, you ought not to run yourself down that way," Hong Diep chided as she hugged her fiancée and kissed him on the cheek. "We are rich in a lot of things money cannot buy—things like health and love and happiness…"

"Speaking of the Japanese…" Hong Diep changed the subject and her tone of voice. "Now that I think of it, I really do not like the way that Japanese sergeant—I believe they call him Moto—looks at me when I bathe in the river. Anyhow, he followed me almost all the way home the other day. I am sure he knows where I live, and I am really afraid he is up to something."

"Hush, Hong Diep. You worry too much about the small things," he said. "Of course Sergeant Moto looks at you when you are bathing. It is the natural thing for a man to do. I would stare too, if I happened to be there. You live up to your name. You really are a beautiful flower."

"You are a bad boy," Hong Diep said as she laughed and pushed Saing Dinh away.

A few minutes after sunset, the happy couple returned to Hong Diep's home. The chilling sight of her father and a widely grinning Sergeant Moto evaporated their smiles in an instant.

As soon as Hong Diep came into the room, her father announced, "Young lady, I have great news for you. Sergeant Moto has paid your dowry in full. You will pack your things and go with him right away. That should make you happy, because your family will soon have our own floating home on the river."

Saing Dinh clenched his fists and said, "No, no. You cannot do that to us. Hong Diep and I are engaged to be married soon. I have most of her dowry money already, and I will have all of it within the next few weeks. You cannot take her from me."

Hong Diep could only gasp and cry.

"Sergeant Moto has paid your dowry in full, and the transaction is completed," her father yelled. "Hong Diep, you will do as you were told. You will pack your things and go immediately with the sergeant. Be up and about it right now, girl—or would you rather I give you another beating?"

Hong Diep did not try to hide her tears of disappointment or her longing looks at Saing Dinh as she left to become Sergeant Moto's personal slave. Saing Dinh's wails echoed eerily from the distance as he walked away in total dejection.

Hong Diep suffered much physical, mental, and sexual abuse from Sergeant Moto with frequent beatings and loud bouts of cursing. He even rationed her food to near starvation quantities. After a couple of months of this torture, she discovered she was pregnant. When she begged the sergeant to give her more food to help her baby grow, he said, "I do not like fat women. Being pregnant makes you look fat enough already."

If she asked his permission to go into town, he threatened her again with his huge fist and yelled, "I do not want you out in public where other men will be gawking at you. I will bring you whatever food and clothing I want you to have."

Slightly more than a month before her baby was born, the Americans dropped bombs on both Hiroshima and Nagasaki, and the Japanese surrendered less than a week later. A few days after that, Sergeant Moto vanished along with all the other Japanese soldiers, as the Japanese pulled out of Cambodia. After ten months of untold torture and near starvation, Hong Diep finally found freedom.

When she returned to her home, far advanced in her pregnancy, only her family members seemed happy to see her. Almost all of her neighbors called her names like "traitor," "turncoat," and "collaborator with the enemy." Even her long-term Vietnamese neighbors, who usually banded together in support of all fellow Vietnamese against the Japanese as well as the Cambodians, turned against her. No one hosted a baby shower for her when her baby was born. One Christian Chinese businesswoman who ran a dry goods business in Battambang did give her a small gift from her store.

Apparently, Hong Diep did not receive any other gift, and the woman became one of the few people she trusted with any of her problems. The businesswoman could speak quite a few words of Japanese because of her business dealings with Japanese soldiers. Hong Diep had learned much of the language from her time with Sergeant Moto. For some reason, the young girl felt free to share all of her feelings with the older woman, but only when they spoke in Japanese. The pair became fast friends.

Because she had been deprived of food when she was pregnant, Hong Diep did not have enough milk to nourish her baby when he was born. Consequently, he cried most of the time if he was not nursing. Her peasant family did not have money to buy extra food for either the baby or his mother, so he did not gain weight. In addition, he developed a large number of festering sores on his head and a few of them scattered over his tiny body.

Totally frustrated with the seemingly hopeless situation, Hong Diep remarked to her mother one day, "Saing Dinh always seemed to know exactly what to do in any situation. If I could just talk to him for a minute, he would advise me about what we should do."

"That reminds me, Hong Diep," her mother said, "when I went to market this morning, I saw Saing Dinh. He wants to come to see you."

"Really, Mama? You actually saw him this morning? Why did you fail to tell me before now? Does he really want to see me?" Hong Diep's face broke into a huge smile for the first time in months.

Hong Diep had been home for several weeks before the news of her return had reached Saing Dinh. He came to visit her at his first chance, and when he saw her, he gasped because she looked so thin and pale. He hugged her tightly and said, "Oh, Hong Diep, I have missed you so much. Every day I asked Buddha to watch over you. I had hoped you might be happy while we were apart, but I can read the answer in your thin face and body. And now they tell me you have a son."

Hong Diep could only cry in answer.

Saing Dinh then reached and took the baby ever so gently from his grandmother's arms. "So this is your son?" he said. "I wish he could be our son, but he is so small and so sickly. I am afraid he could never survive our trip."

Hong Diep looked up and her sobbing ceased. "But why do you say he cannot be our son?" she shrieked wide-eyed and angry. "And what is this trip you are speaking about? You have never said anything to me about us taking a trip."

"I had hoped we could get married right away and go to Thailand. They tell me we could find plenty of work there. The way most Cambodians hate all Vietnamese, we will never make much of a living here. And now that your neighbors have turned so hard against my beautiful Hong Diep…" Saing Dinh's voice cracked, and he hesitated for a moment before he said, "We could be so much happier and so much better off if we were away from this place."

"Oh, Saing Dinh," Hong Diep said, "that sounds so romantic."

"In one way, it would be romantic because we would finally be together," he continued. "On the other hand, it would be really tragic because we cannot take the baby with us. He is far too small and too weak, and you do not have enough milk to feed him. He could never survive a trip of that length, especially since we will have to walk.

That will be hard enough on you and me. From the way he looks right now, I believe he will die even if you stay here and try to take care of him."

Hong Diep's face turned ashen white as she said, "But, Saing Dinh, you know I could never leave my baby."

"Think of it this way, Hong Diep," Saing Dinh said. "If you stay at home and try to take care of him, he will probably die anyhow. Then you and I will have forever lost any chance for a life together. I am sure you have seen many of these starving kids with sores on their heads and bodies in your lifetime. How many of them have you ever known to survive?

"Both you and the baby would be better off if you gave up this fight right now and let him die. You can tell how bad his suffering is by the way he cries all the time, and I can see that you trying so hard to feed him is pulling you down. You are putting your own life in grave danger by what you are doing, and he will probably die even if you keep up this folly."

Saing Dinh's voice had reached an evangelistic pitch by this time. "Give it up. Let him go. He will be out of his misery, and you and I can finally get married. He will be a winner and so will we. He will not suffer any more, and we can go to Thailand where we can be together and—" Saing Dinh broke off.

"But I cannot make the choice for you," he said. "You must choose between him and me. If you choose him, it will mean possible death for both of you. If you choose me, it will mean a chance at a new and better life in Thailand, and he will be out of his misery. You and only you can make that choice—but it seems to me you really have only one choice. I will be waiting to see what decision you make."

"But Saing Dinh, it is so hard to choose. I love you both so very much, and I know so little about babies and about real life. Do you honestly believe my baby does not have a chance to live and that he is suffering so much he would be better off dead?" Hong Diep said between her sobs.

"I am not a doctor, but the way he looks makes me think he is well on his way to death already. Just take a good look at all those boils on his head and over his body. Every one of those sores is pouring poison into his tiny body. How can he fight off all of that infection and get them healed when he is slowly starving to death?"

"Can I have a little more time to think about it?"

"Not much more, my dear. We cannot afford to wait very long. The rainy season will start soon, and it is not safe for us to be on the road during the monsoons. I will come back tomorrow to hear your decision." Saing Dinh headed for the door.

Hong Diep did not sleep a wink as she wrestled with her decision and listened to her baby's hungry cries, in spite of her almost constant effort to feed him. As she tossed and turned, she reached a decision that it would be better for her baby and for her, if she followed Saing Dinh's advice to give up the fight to save his life.

The couple married in a civil ceremony the next morning. Later that afternoon, they packed their meager belongings into a large, homemade two-wheel cart. Very early the following morning, Hong Diep kissed her baby good-bye on the banks of the Sangker River. Then she gently placed his thin, sore-riddled body in a community garbage can in an enclosure behind Wat Bovil. With that distasteful act behind them, the newlyweds were off on their honeymoon journey to Thailand.

"It is by far the hardest thing I ever had to do," Hong Diep said to her new husband as she left her baby, "but I honestly believe he and I will both be better off."

The route the newlyweds chose to take as they started toward Thailand passed by the home of the businesswoman who had befriended Hong Diep. The woman happened to be in her garden picking green tea leaves and eggplant for her family's dinner when she saw and recognized Hong Diep. She rushed to the roadside to speak to her friend.

"Hong Diep," she said. "I am so happy to see you. I have been worried almost sick about you and your baby, and I have been praying for both of you. Where might you two be heading with your cart so full this early in the morning? And how is the baby?"

Hong Diep forced a smile and said "Saing Dinh and I got married yesterday. We are on our way to Thailand to begin a new life together. There is so little work in Cambodia, and it pays so poorly, we do not believe we can ever make a reasonable living here. Folks tell us there is plenty of work there … Besides that, you know how most people in Cambodia feel about all Vietnamese, and you of all people know how badly my neighbors have treated me ever since I came back home."

As Hong Diep spoke, the woman's eyes searched every inch of their cart. When she saw no evidence of a baby or any of the things you need to care for a baby, she demanded, "If you are moving to Thailand, then where is your baby?"

Hong Diep started to cry and confessed to her friend exactly what they had done and why they had done it. The woman screamed and said, "Oh my God, no. Please tell me exactly where the garbage can that you left him in is located."

"It is the one in the enclosure directly behind Wat Bovil," Hong Diep managed to say between her loud sobs.

The woman threw down her tea leaves and eggplant and did not ask any further questions. Only one thought occupied her mind. She had to get to Wat Bovil.

Hong Diep called out to her friend as she sped away. "He will be much better off when he is dead and out of his misery. I did everything I could possibly do for him, and I could not bear to just watch him die in spite of everything."

The woman ran as fast as her legs could carry her. As she darted through the streets of Battambang, she prayed and asked God for strength and speed and for the baby to stay alive until she could reach him. As she ran, her mind raced faster than her feet: *What if someone gets there before I do? What if they put in some heavy garbage on top of him and suffocate him?*

When she reached the garbage can and lifted its lid, the odor of rotten fish almost overwhelmed her. Someone had thrown a few old fish heads on top of the baby. *Surely they did not hear his crying*, she thought. *It is so weak, I can barely hear the smallest grunt, and I know he is here.*

When she spotted the motionless baby, her heart sank. So many biting flies covered his body that he appeared almost black. She picked him up and pulled up her gardening apron to cover him. Then she ran as fast as she could to find the wife of the local American missionary who knew something about nursing. She felt certain a missionary would know what to do in a situation like this.

The American woman helped her clean up the baby and she poured peroxide on his boils. "That will help fight infection," she said. Then she bound up his head with gauze and healing ointment and put bandages on the sores on his body. She told the woman about a mother nearby who was still nursing her baby and had so much milk she had to pump extra milk from her breasts each time her baby finished nursing. That mother agreed to serve as a wet nurse and feed the sick baby twice a day.

The businesswoman took the baby into her home and raised him as her God-given child. His weight picked up right away and his general health improved slowly, but it took two long years to get his boils healed.

SamSan could not hold his tongue any longer. "Let me guess," he said to his mother, "I am the baby in that story."

His mother replied, "Yes, SamSan, my visitor just now was Hong Diep, your natural mother. You are the baby that came so close to dying in that garbage can. I am the woman who rescued you, and Mrs. Allison is the missionary lady who helped us save your life."

"Where does my birth mother live now?" he asked.

"She lives with her family in Wat Tana, Thailand. It is a tiny village near the city of Aranyaprathet."

His mother ended her story by saying, "That is the true story of the miraculous way God saved your life and brought you into our family. You are not our child by chance. You are our child by choice."

SamSan glanced over at me and said, "Mother told me that story many times, and she always ended it with 'You are our child by choice.' How much of her story is based on fact and how much is a figment of her imagination, I cannot be certain, but my birth mother confirmed much of it when I finally had the chance to visit her in 1974.

"I believe God saved my life through Mother's efforts. Even if I had survived the garbage can, she saved me from the nearly hopeless life of a half-breed Vietnamese peasant orphan in Cambodia—something almost as bad as death. From that time on, I started a journey into an entirely different lifestyle. I came into a Christian home that was affluent compared to my old home but certainly not rich.

"It was like Moses being pulled from the bulrushes and taken to Pharaoh's palace by Pharaoh's daughter but on a much smaller scale."

The Family (and the Story) Grows
Winder-Barrow Hospital

L & D waiting room—8:00 pm, March 17, 1982

Keng had borne two sons to SamSan while they were in Cambodia, but the first of them had died shortly after birth. A few months after their arrival in Winder almost two years earlier, I had delivered a third child for the couple. During all this time, I still had gleaned little additional information about SamSan's life in Cambodia. I had not pressed him hard for information, because he still feared for the life of his lost son. When Keng's labor pains were well established, she entered the local hospital for me to deliver this baby also. Shortly after her admission, my examination showed her labor to be in its early stages, and there were no obvious complications.

While the nurses cared for Keng in the labor room, I took a seat with the family in the waiting room to keep them company and to reassure them as we whiled away the waiting hours. SamSan muttered aloud to himself and tears welled in his eyes as he paced back and forth across the carpeted floor. It might have been selfish, but the thought occurred to me that he needed something to distract him from this state of agitation. This appeared to be the perfect time for me to hear more of his story, so I pulled an empty chair alongside mine and motioned for him to sit.

"SamSan," I said to the wide-eyed and shaking expectant father, "You might as well sit down. I checked Keng just a few minutes ago, and it looks like her delivery is anywhere from two to six hours away. She is doing well and so is the baby. Pacing the floor will only wear your shoes and the hospital's carpet out before your baby gets here. The nurses will keep a close watch on her for us and they will call me when she is ready to deliver. This is a good time for you and me to have a long talk."

SamSan forced a smile that looked more like a grimace as he honored my request. He sat on the edge of the chair and nervously crossed and uncrossed his legs. His look of anxiety returned as he asked, "Do you think she will be all right?"

"There is no doubt in my mind about it," I said to him. "My examination showed no sign of any problem. Our nurses are good, and they will be right on top of the situation every minute. They will let me know if even the smallest problem comes up."

My words of reassurance had the desired effect, and SamSan appeared more relaxed. "In the meanwhile, this looks like a great opportunity for me to learn some things about you," I said.

"What do you want to know?" he asked with an unexpected eagerness.

"I have often wondered why your parents chose to give you the name, SamSan. Did it have some special significance to them?"

A trace of a smile spread across his face as he pondered and finally gave an answer. "My parents had big dreams for me when they adopted me in spite of the fact that I was tiny, sickly, and weak. They knew the odds against my survival were very high, but they wanted me to grow up big and strong. Because they were Christians, it seemed only natural that they should name me after Samson, the strongest man in the Bible.

"But almost nobody in my family ever called me by my Christian name. Most of them used my nickname, *Peing*, a Chinese word that means 'peace.' They nicknamed me Peing because my birth date came very close to the time when peace came to Cambodia after World War Two."

His quick and detailed answer gave me the feeling of having an open door, so I pressed on. "Right now, it will do you good to have your mind on something other than Keng's labor. That makes this a perfect time for you to tell me everything about your childhood years after your parents adopted you. It is hard for me to believe any harm could come to your family in Cambodia if you told that part of your story after this long a time. After all, you have been an adult for nearly twenty years. I want to know every detail of how you came to be the man you are today," I said, hoping he would feel comfortable sharing his story.

SamSan frowned and appeared in deep thought for several seconds before he gave a response. "It has been a long time since anyone should have thought of me as a child," he finally began. "And I really cannot think of any possible way my son could be harmed by my telling that part of my story now."

With that statement, he leaned back in his chair and seemed to relax more completely. As he became involved in telling his story, he no longer appeared startled or turned frantically toward the labor room door with every moan that filtered through the thick hospital walls or at the sight of every nurse who flitted back and forth through the waiting room. I settled back expectantly and jotted down occasional notes as he began to speak:

"After my adoption, nothing that happened to me during my childhood seemed unusual for a Chinese boy in Cambodia at the time."

"But you are not Chinese," I objected. "You told me your father was Japanese and your mother Vietnamese."

He smiled at my ignorance and patiently explained, "Yes, I know, but my adoptive parents were Chinese immigrants in Cambodia, so the government classified me as Chinese.

"As I was saying, very little that happened to me as a boy seemed unusual at the time. However, some of the ordinary things that did occur prepared me for events and trials that came later in my life. Some of those happenings might have even saved my life. Those are the things I want to tell you about, because I believe they show how God had His hand on my life even that early."

By this time, SamSan appeared oblivious to routine activity of his hospital surroundings as he became completely engrossed in telling at least a portion of his story, a pleasure he had been denied for many years. Details had been what I requested, so he began a soliloquy that covered several areas of his younger life in surprising detail.

SamSan's Account of His Youth

Battambang, Cambodia—1946–1967

My adoptive parents were Ly Kon Nong and Chan Su Ho. In Cambodia, the family name is stated first and the wife does not take on the husband's family name. Each of them operated a small sales booth in the community market of Battambang. My father's stand dealt mostly in nonperishable grocery items such as salt, rice, sugar, and spices. He also carried a few semi-perishable things like hot peppers, onions, and garlic. I helped him by gathering the hot peppers, garlic, and onions from the garden and getting them ready for sale. Once in a while, I ran his store for an hour or so while he did other things. I looked forward to those times. It made me feel grown-up.

Mom ran a small dry goods operation. She sold inexpensive cloth, sewing supplies like needles, thread, and thimbles, plus a few different kinds of home supplies. Most of the time she had some very fine silk for sale. I wanted to help her, but I never knew enough about her merchandise to manage her stand completely even for a short time. She occasionally asked me to watch the merchandise while she ran an errand.

My parents were not rich people by any stretch of the imagination, but we never seemed to lack for anything. They raised three children besides me—a boy and two girls—and they adopted all four of us. Our parents loved us deeply, but they were strict and demanded that we live by the highest Christian principles.

I was sixteen years younger than my brother, Chong Ky, so our relationship never seemed particularly close. Before I remember anything, he had enrolled in Bible school and was rarely at home. I was four years older than Marilyn, the older of my two sisters, and the baby, Kim, was three years younger than Marilyn. In spite of the differences in our ages—or perhaps it was *because* of the differences—we got along fairly well. I believe God placed me in that home.

The day Mother pulled me out of the garbage can, she carried me directly to Mrs. Allison's house. After that, Mrs. Allison had me to come to her house every day or two to get my boils treated. That went on for more than two years before the sores finally healed. By that time, I had become a regular playmate with John, Paul, and Helen—the Allison children. At times, they seemed closer to me than my own family. I almost believed I was an American.

When I played with the Allison children, we carried on our conversations in English, but when I went home we spoke only Chinese. In public places, I heard and spoke Khmer and French. By the time I started school, I had developed a small vocabulary in all four languages, so it was only natural that language should become my hobby and later be my profession.

As I grew older and wanted to practice my language skills, I went into town to look for Westerners. When I spotted someone with a western look, I would ask him or her, "Do you speak English? Parlez vous Francaise?"

Most of the time, English- or French-speaking tourists seemed glad to hear their native language spoken in a far-off place. It certainly made me happy when they responded in either language. By answering their questions about Battambang and/or Cambodia or by giving them directions, I had a chance to develop my language skills. Then I felt free to ask them questions about their homeland to advance my knowledge of the world. Although I never made a charge for any information I gave, they would sometimes give me a tip. I looked on it as a win-win situation for both of us.

Even during my childhood, I suppose you could call me a capitalist living in a part of the world that leaned toward communism. I always looked for a way to earn a few extra riels. At an early age, maybe ten or twelve, I wanted to earn my own money, so my parents helped me arrange to buy bread from a local baker and sell it in the city. I paid the baker thirty-five riels for fifty small loaves and sold them for one riel each. The baker agreed to return my money for any loaves I could not sell, so I knew I would not lose. I sold bread all over the city of Battambang from a basket on top of my head. I usually made about twenty-five riels a day, equal to about twenty-three cents in American money, but it seemed like a lot to a child.

In America, you have a saying, "A penny saved is a penny earned." I lived by that rule and saved my money. I would do almost anything within legal and moral limits to make a little pocket money. When I got into high school, I even taught a private class in English for seven or eight paying students. One of my students worked as a watch repairman, and I traded him English lessons for watch-making lessons, hoping I could make a bit of extra money by repairing watches. For a long time, I felt cheated because not one single paying customer ever wanted me to touch his watch. A few years later, that knowledge certainly paid huge dividends for me.

"How?" I questioned, on the edge of my seat.

"I had better not go into that at this time," he replied.

His response disappointed me, as I was eager to learn more about how he had become the intelligent, confident man who sat before me. Just as I was about to press the issue, there was a sharp cry from the labor room.

"Don't worry," I reassured him. "If Keng has any kind of problem, they will let me know right away."

He nodded and smiled slightly, but his uneasy squirming clearly showed an unsettled spirit. "Before we go on," he said, "may we say a prayer for Keng? I cannot help but worry a little bit about her."

"Certainly," I agreed, and we bowed our heads together. By the time he voiced his "amen" in Chinese, I had a new question ready for him.

"Then tell me about your Christian faith," I said eagerly. "I understand that less than one percent of the Cambodian population is Christian."

9:15 pm

"Yes, we Christians were certainly in the minority. As for me, I cannot remember ever not being a believer, although my baptism did not come until I was eight. Every member of my family had a strong Christian faith, and we went to church every Sunday to hear Rev. Allison preach. Most of the time we also attended services in the middle of the week.

"Mrs. Allison and Rev. Samuel Mok, an associate Chinese pastor in our church, were my Sunday school teachers. Mother served as their substitute. Our teacher would occasionally read a printed story to us and show us colored pictures from the book. More often, they simply told us stories from the Bible and gave us cut-out pictures from old American Christian magazines or from Christmas cards. We collected those pictures avidly, because nothing in Cambodia equaled them. From the pictures, and from knowing the Allisons, I visualized America as a perfect place where every person lived a Christian life and did what was right. Almost every night, I dreamed about coming here.

"When I was very small, Mrs. Allison taught us a song for one of our special children's programs. It is called 'Bringing in the Sheaves.' I still remember the words of the song and its tune. I even remember the hand motions she taught us to do while we sang it.

Sowing in the morning, sowing seeds of kindness;
Sowing in the noontide and the dewy eve;
Waiting for the harvest and the time of reaping,
We shall come rejoicing bringing in the sheaves.
Bringing in the sheaves; bringing in the sheaves
We shall come rejoicing bringing in the sheaves.
Bringing in the sheaves; bringing in the sheaves
We shall come rejoicing bringing in the sheaves.

He grinned broadly, apparently pleased with his memory of the entire performance. By this time, he seemed completely oblivious to the hospital surroundings and totally involved in the moment as he returned to his story:

At times, we endured persecution because of our Christian faith. Most of the problems came about as we sat in the open-air auditorium of the church. Sometimes, a number of students from the Chinese school would gather outside to jeer at us. Then, if someone in the congregation responded in a way that made them angry, they threw things like rotten tomatoes or even small stones at us. That always made me mad, and I wanted to fight, but my parents told me, "Son, we must pray for them. Most of their teachers follow Chairman Mao's brand of communism, and they teach them that all religions are false. They are simply following what their teachers are telling them—and you must remember that Jesus taught us to 'turn the other cheek.'"

Before that time, politics had never affected me personally, so I had paid little attention to political things. Now, I began to notice that, even though Prince Sihanouk claimed to run a neutral government, he inched closer and closer to the support of Chairman Mao. As communism grew stronger in Cambodia, the pressure on Americans, especially on Christian Americans, grew more intense.

Demonstrations against our church became uglier and more frequent, and those against the United States caused a virtual shutdown of the US Embassy.

Prince Sihanouk apparently became paranoid that the United States was trying to overthrow him. He began to consider all American missionaries as CIA agents and, therefore, his enemies. He decreed that Buddhism was the official religion of Cambodia and placed strict controls on all Christian congregations. Because of the danger to the lives of Rev. Allison and his family, the CMA (Christian and Missionary Alliance) church board recalled them to the United States. I felt almost like an orphan again. I ignored the fact that people would classify me as an American sympathizer and went to the USIS (United States Information Service) to continue my study of English.

During this time, church meetings had to be held in private homes. One night, the police raided a meeting my family held in our home and arrested fifteen or twenty of us. It nearly frightened me to death, but they released me and all the other children almost immediately because of our youth. They agreed to release any adult who would denounce their faith in Christ. Most of the members, including my parents, refused to do this, but Rev. Chan Ouch, one of our associate pastors, almost immediately promised to quit preaching, and they let him go.

The police held my parents for about two months, but they were not physically as rough on them as they were on the pastors. They tortured Rev. Mok and Evangelist Sem Bun with thumb screws and in some other ways the pastors would never tell me about. I will never forget the disfigurement of Rev. Bun's hands and the difference in his voice when he returned to the church.

I cooked food every day and carried it to my parents in the prison. When they finally came back home, our worship services consisted of a few of us getting together in secret to listen to forbidden Bible broadcasts in the Khmer language that came on the radio from America. It was a very frightening—but exciting—experience for the children.

But Christians were not the only victims of discrimination. Cambodians hated all Vietnamese and looked for ways to harm them. The discrimination did not seem nearly as severe for Chinese outsiders as it did for Vietnamese, but it was there. They tolerated us, but their treatment of the Vietnamese appeared so bad to me that it caused me to worry they might start a revolution. Government rules perpetuated this intense racial prejudice and segregation. Outsiders could not legally own property in Cambodia, nor could the Cambodian government employ them legally in any capacity. Not only that, but they could not hold political office even if they had been born in Cambodia or if they had lived there for fifty or more years. A person could buy his citizenship if he knew the right people and paid bribes to them, but theoretically, no outsider could ever become a citizen.

The segregated and unequal school system was the thing that caused me so many personal and practical problems. The inequality bothered me more than the segregation because it directly affected my education. The government classified all students by race, and each student wore a uniform that identified his school. Because my adoptive family was Chinese, they assigned me to the Chinese school.

Unfortunately, public education for all Chinese students went only through the seventh grade, and the school did not teach any of its classes in Khmer, the official language of Cambodia. For that reason, I, and most of the ethnic Chinese in Cambodia at the time, could not read or write Khmer, and most of us spoke the language very poorly. In contrast, Cambodian students got daily instruction in both French and in Khmer, and their schools offered a full twelve-year program.

As a child in elementary school, my studies had not seemed very important to me. I preferred to play children's games like jump rope, tag, and hide-and-seek—but soccer really became my passion. I performed fairly well in soccer and developed a lifelong love for it.

When I got to middle school, I became more interested in academics and set higher goals for myself, especially in language courses, but I still played soccer. By that time, I fully understood my need for more education than the system provided. It worried me a lot that I would not be able to advance to high school.

My parents shared my concern about my education and enrolled me in a private Chinese high school. In this school, my life suddenly became more of a dilemma because every teacher appeared to be communist. They tried to convince each student that religion was a myth and a pipe dream. Their arguments were so convincing they caused even me to lean toward communism during the school week. I felt truly guilty about it, knowing the problems the communists had caused our church and, especially, what they had done to the Allisons.

But when I heard those communist teachings refuted every Sunday at church and again each summer when I attended Bible camp, my desire to be a good Christian returned. I felt like a Yo-Yo, pulled back and forth. I even began to think of religion as a sort of lottery where, if you had the right number at the right moment, you would be okay. Otherwise, you had to take your chances.

Before that, I had never done anything worse than cut one day of Bible camp to go see my uncle; but I am really ashamed of some of the things I did during those days. I felt angry and confused, but I did not feel physically strong enough to defend myself. Therefore, I decided to study martial arts.

When Kaing Hai Leng (*Kaing Hai Leng* means "sea dragon" in Cambodian) did a Kung Fu demonstration in Battambang, it made a big impression on me. He lay down on a bed of nails and told me to jump from about four or five feet onto his belly. When I did, he only laughed and rose up to give a thrilling Kung Fu demonstration. After that, he sold his exclusive tonic elixir that he claimed as the source of his amazing strength, endurance, and quickness.

I asked him to give me instructions in Kung Fu, and he accepted me as a student. After a few lessons, he said to me and two other of his most zealous students, "Before you can consider yourself to be a real man, you must be able to face death head on—even be able to stare it in the face. Tonight's test will determine how well you can do that."

That night, he drove us to the Chinese cemetery and gave us a hammer, a pry-bar, a large rice sack, a candle, and a map to a certain grave site. He knew the person buried in that bier belonged to a large family of ancestor worshippers, and they had placed large amounts of jewelry and money in the bier for their mother's use in the future life.

"Pry the lid off the concrete bier and you will see a lot of money and jewelry in there," he said. "Put all of it in the sack and bring it to me. Be absolutely quiet and do not get caught in the act of taking the stuff. That is the only way you could ever get into trouble."

When we told him we were worried about the family members calling the police when they found the bier open, he said, "Do not worry about the family. When they see the top is open, they will be happy because they will think, *Mama's spirit rose up and took all those things with her. She should be really happy now, and our gifts will help her in her new life.*"

When we opened that bier, I vomited because of the horrible smell—so did one of the other students. It took me four or five days to wash the odor from my hands. Mr. Sea Dragon said our throwing up proved we were not tough enough yet. He made us rob three or four more graves before we got up enough nerve to tell him we would not do that again. I never dreamed those experiences would prepare me for some horrible things I would see later in life.

When I completed the Chinese high school, I felt it had failed to advance my education, so I spoke to my parents about that. This time, they consulted Rev. Chan Ouch, who suggested that he should legally adopt me. "As my adopted son, SamSan would have all the rights of a Cambodian citizen and could go to the Cambodian high school, which is much better," he said, "and it would open up other doors for him later on in life."

Rev. Ouch went to his home village, a very small place called Chondoeu Swar (which means "where the monkey climbs the tree").

He found a local official there who, for a bribe of five thousand riels, would provide a birth certificate for me. My parents paid the bribe money and got the false paper. With the registration of my fake birth certificate in 1962, I became a "legal" citizen of Cambodia with all its rights and privileges. At that time, my name officially changed from Ly SamSan to Ouch SamSan, but, as a Cambodian citizen, I could finally get the quality education I needed.

I got off to a slow start in the Cambodian high school. In fact, I failed the first year because I had not had any instruction in the Khmer language before that time. I could read a few words of Khmer, but I could not write it, and my spoken Khmer was only the street language. However, after I got the hang of reading, I managed very well. When I graduated from high school, a small Chinese school recruited me as their teacher of English and elementary French. Finally, at age twenty-one, I had a respectable job because I had at long last received the education I needed.

Bribery was an everyday fact of life for most people in Cambodia, but I hated it with a passion, and it bothered me a great deal that my parents had participated in that corrupt process for my sake. However, I certainly enjoyed the wonderful results it produced for me. One of the things it did was to clear the way for me to become a government employee in the future. I believe God had a direct hand in that too.

When Rev. Allison finally came back to Cambodia in early 1963, he seemed very happy to see me. He asked me to go on a home visit with him some distance from Battambang. On our way back home, he complained of severe tiredness. When he stopped the car, I noticed his breathing was hard and fast, and he was sweating heavily. He laid his head on the steering wheel, and when I called to him, he did not answer. I ran to a nearby rice mill for help. Someone carried me by motorcycle to Battambang to notify his wife, but we could not do anything for him. He died before help could arrive.

The next day, an airplane from the US Embassy came to pick up Rev. Allison's body. They even brought a casket to place him in that was supposed to be used only in case of the death of the Ambassador to Cambodia. It really impressed me that Americans would care so much for their citizens they would actually send a plane after their mission-ary's body and supply him with a casket. I wanted even more to go there.

I had never been very close to an airplane on the ground before that time, and it really excited me to get on board. I asked the pilots to teach me to fly, but they informed me I had to study a number of things first. I wanted to go to the United States, and I wanted to learn to fly.

Another Son

12:05 am, March 18, 1982

About this time, the obstetrical nurse motioned for me to come to the delivery room. Thirty minutes later, I returned to let SamSan get a glimpse of his latest, very healthy, screaming son.

"How is Keng?" he asked while tears streamed down his cheek.

"She is fine," I responded. Only then did he offer to take his newborn son from my hands.

The family chose the Christian name of John for this child, in honor of the writer of the Gospel. This continued the tradition they had begun when they named their first son David, in honor of the biblical king, and their second son Samuel, in honor of the biblical prophet.

More than fifteen years passed in which my contact with SamSan was sporadic, and he revealed only tantalizing tidbits about his life in Cambodia. In the meantime, he secured different employment that allowed him more free time. He indicated to me that the situation in Cambodia had changed to the point that he now felt free to talk but, by this time, he had become deaf to the point that every question had to be written. I began a series of after-work formal interviews once or twice a week, jotting down notes and recording some of the interviews on tape. These one or two hour sessions continued for nearly six months.

THE MAN EMERGES
Battambang, Cambodia—
mid 1968

SamSan's twenty-second birthday approached, and Cambodian custom demanded that his parents arrange a marriage for him. They wanted their son's life partner to be a Christian, but their church roll did not include a suitable female prospect, and no other Christian congregation existed in Battambang. His mother spoke to her best friend, Lor Heng, and asked, "What kind of dowry would you expect if SamSan were to marry your daughter, Noy?"

Lor Heng responded, "Dear, dear Su Ho. Even though you are my best friend, I will never give my consent for any of my daughters to marry your son. Although it is a selfish reason, I have a very good reason for that decision, and dowry has nothing to do with it.

"If Noy should marry SamSan, she would probably follow your family tradition and become a Christian. Then, she would forget about her responsibilities to her old Buddhist mother and she would never give me the reverence I am due from my daughter. When I am dead, I want Noy to light every candle and burn every kind of incense I am due. I also want her to say every prayer and place every meal I should have placed at my grave. I do love you dearly, and I am sure it is selfish of me, but no amount of dowry could gain my consent for your son to marry any daughter of mine."

Every inquiry the family made outside of their church about a prospective bride brought up the matter of religious difference. His parent's search continued to prove fruitless until Su Ho enlisted the help of Rev. Samuel Mok. Rev. Mok, a Chinese co-pastor of their church in Battambang, had been SamSan's Sunday school teacher for many years. He felt beholden to Su Ho because she had lobbied one of the richest men in Battambang a few years earlier and had negotiated permission for her co-pastor to marry the rich man's daughter.

Rev. Mok soon noted that SamSan made wistful glances at the new nanny for the Mok children, Nai Guek. This young Chinese farm girl had come into the city to care for Rev. Mok's rapidly expanding family. Under the Mok family's influence, Guek had recently made a profession of faith in Christ, and the pastor baptized her into church membership. Su Ho chided herself because, as the newest member of the local church congregation, Guek had escaped her constantly searching eye. SamSan's embarrassed mother prayed for forgiveness for her faithless, frantic search and for her failure to see the answer that God had provided right under her nose.

Rev. Mok helped SamSan's parents arrange with Guek's parents for the couple to be married. They scheduled the wedding to take place in early January 1969, a few days after SamSan completed his one-year contract as a schoolteacher. The marriage contract met with SamSan's wholehearted approval.

A Christian wedding in Cambodia consists of two parts and is an all-day affair. There is a formal religious ceremony held in the church building early in the morning and a secular, raucous celebration in the evening.

The religious portion of SamSan's nuptials featured the tradition-heavy and ritualistic, short marriage ceremony with only family members in attendance. The church looked very pretty, decorated with flowers from his mother's garden.

SamSan thought Guek looked beautiful, arrayed in her simple, long, white silk dress made from the best material from his mother's store. He really liked the hand bouquet she carried. His mother had fashioned it using jasmine and gardenias fresh from her garden.

SamSan squirmed uneasily in his black business suit and white tie throughout the entire ceremony. He could hardly wait until the entire process concluded.

His parents made the evening dinner and celebration a gala affair held under a red, yellow, and blue canvas tent well over a hundred feet long. More than two hundred guests attended the festivities that included all the amenities and pageantry of a first-class Cambodian wedding: beautiful banners, hung tastefully on each wall wished good fortune for the newlyweds and their guests.

The colorful costumes worn by hostesses in each area and the fabulous food served in that section represented different portions of Cambodia. Lavish lanterns that depicted oriental mythology with dragons, warriors, and beautiful Asian women shed bright light on each area, with the exception of the space reserved for dancing to melodious music provided by professional musicians.

In keeping with the family's Christian beliefs, they served no alcohol and, unfortunately, many wedding guests became angry. The disenchanted guests chorused their disappointment to the bridegroom.

"You are acting like a cheapskate by not serving us any beer or wine. Therefore, we will give you only half of our usual gifts for newlyweds."

SamSan smiled a large, fake smile and bowed appropriately to the group as he made his apology. "Surely, you can understand that we need to follow our church's teachings. Most of you follow the teachings of Buddha. We try to follow the teachings of Jesus Christ, and our church teaches us to refrain from alcohol."

Unimpressed with their host's explanation, most of the guests kept their word and reduced their gifts of money, a tradition in Cambodia. SamSan had counted on that money to provide extras for their honeymoon and their housing start. Now they would simply have to make do with less. However, it grieved him deeply that even the happy occasion of his wedding had been marred by the tendency of Cambodians to misunderstand and persecute Christian believers.

A New Career

It had only taken one year of classroom teaching to convince SamSan that he had not found his life's calling in the teaching profession. He had quite a few reasons for that decision. The primary one was that he would never be able to support a wife on the pay he received, and the work had become far too demanding of his time. Furthermore, most of his students did not seem to appreciate his efforts to advance their educations because they felt the subjects he taught, English and French, would never be of any significant importance in their lives. Now that he had a wife, he definitely needed to find a new profession.

After a short honeymoon in Phnom Penh, the couple embarked on an unusual business venture. They began importing durian into Battambang from the jungles of Cambodia. Durian, a very expensive fruit, is also called "thorn fruit" and "king of fruits." A single durian can cost as much as fifty American dollars. A very large and ominously spiny fruit that may be oblong or round, each durian may weigh up to seven pounds and may vary in color from green to brown. It bears no resemblance to any American or European fruit.

Like strong cheeses in Europe, the smell, as well as the taste, of durian is either adored or abhorred by individuals in the Asian population. In addition, many people in Cambodia claim that durian is "very good for the stomach," and they use it strictly for medicinal purposes.

Durian only grows in the hard-to-reach, densest jungles of Cambodia, Thailand, and Vietnam. Because no roads or bridges existed in the area where the durian trees grew, a person could only bring the fruit out of the jungles by elephant.

"Guek and I made the trek from Battambang to Sam Lot village and back to Battambang every week by either truck or bus," SamSan said. "A round trip from Battambang took three or four days. It panned out to be extremely hazardous and tiring work, but it was exciting.

"While I rode an elephant into the jungle to gather durian, Guek stayed in the village with friends. My income more than doubled from what my school teacher's salary had been. Just as importantly, I learned a lot about jungle survival tactics—especially about which plants were poisonous and which ones a person could safely eat. Moreover, I believe I learned every technique that existed for climbing trees—barefoot, wearing shoes with and without climbers attached, and using ropes. Those skills would be very helpful to me later in my life.

"One time when I was about to reach for a durian I had spotted, I came face-to-face with a twin-barred tree snake. I had heard of these snakes—that they were beautiful—but he did not look beautiful to me at that moment. I also knew their bite would probably not kill a person, but it could make one very sick, and here I was deep in the jungle. Apparently, our chance meeting frightened him as much as it did me, and he flattened out his body and launched himself from the tree. You cannot imagine the relief I felt as he glided to the ground."

After three months of importing durian, SamSan heard that a small, new, insurgent guerrilla band known as the CPK (Communist Party of Kampuchea, the same group that Prince Sihanouk would later dub the Khmer Rouge) had killed a rice merchant in the area of the jungle where he gathered durian. "It is not worth the risk of dying to be in the durian business," he said to Guek. "It is time for us to move to Phnom Penh and look for another line of work."

SamSan Finds His Calling

In Phnom Penh, the couple closely scrutinized every help-wanted ad they could find in both the newspapers and the magazines. One particular magazine advertisement for a tourist agency called SOKHAR Voyages (Société Khmère des Auberges Royales) appeared quite promising. The ad said, "Wanted: Cambodian citizens who speak fluent English and/or French to become SOKHAR tour guides."

"That is it," SamSan said. He did not attempt to contain his excitement about this opportunity they had stumbled across. He knew that the royal family of Cambodia owned and operated SOKHAR Voyages. That meant the agency functioned as an official operation of the Cambodian government. Therefore, employees of SOKHAR Voyages were considered as government employees and would garner all of the lucrative benefits of such employment.

"That is the job I have spent my entire life training for without knowing it," he excitedly said to Guek. "As much as I hated the fact that my parents had to certify a lie and pay a bribe to obtain my Cambodian citizenship, I might as well not even apply for this job if they had not done that for me. God certainly does work in mysterious ways, just as the Bible says."

The manager of the tourist agency seemed almost as excited as SamSan when the expert linguist appeared the following morning to make application for a job. "We do not have a guide who speaks ten languages," he exclaimed. "I want you to take our language tests today."

The oral and written examinations seemed elementary to SamSan, and he passed all of them with ease. After only a brief orientation, the company put him to work immediately, and he began guiding tours in French or English throughout Phnom Penh and the areas immediately surrounding the city.

SamSan proved to be a natural for the tour guide business and a lightning-quick study of every detail of the area around Phnom Penh. He almost immediately learned the history of each significant building, each fountain, every statue, and most streets in the area. In addition, he could soon identify and discuss the dominant nationality of the citizenry in each sector of the city as well as the preponderant type of business in each general area.

Because the royal family owned the tourist agency and some of them actually worked there, he soon became good friends with Prince Norodom Yuvaneath, son of Prince Sihanouk, the ruler of Cambodia. He also worked with Prince Norodom Pheanureak, nephew of Prince Sihanouk, as well as Princess Norodom Danin, Sihanouk's niece and the wife of Jimmy Jacks, a pilot with a civilian airline in Cambodia. The quintet became very close friends and developed a great respect for one another.

Every day, as he guided tours of the Royal Palace with its opulent architecture, its historic statues, and the pomp and ceremony of the palace guard, SamSan indulged his guests with both humorous and informative chatter. He explained the significance of each architectural feature of the palace and of each statue. He gave a detailed reason for every part of the uniforms worn by the highly acclaimed palace guard and for each piece of equipment used by them. He also explained every precise ceremonial movement made by the guard members.

During a tour of the palace, there occasionally came the serendipity of a glimpse of a royal family member. The popular tour guide had totally familiarized himself with the name, exact title, and assigned functions of every person in that famous family. When a spotting of royalty occurred, he could immediately share that information with his guests in colorful detail and with great flourish.

At the Royal Palace Theater, where the *Apsara* (Royal dancers) regaled in their intricate, colorful costumes, he pointed out that each dancer represented a supernaturally beautiful celestial nymph of Buddhist mythology. The dancers, who danced to the music of their fallen hero husbands, symbolized female spirits of the clouds and waters, and each of their colorful costumes represented a different aspect of the performing arts. He also explained the meaning of most of their graceful dance maneuvers, many of which cast mystical allusion to the ancient myth that the Apsara could change their shapes at will, and he never failed to mention the beauty, grace, and elegance of the individual dancers.

Because of his large vocabulary and the interest he took in his guests, he quickly became a favorite of both management and tourists. The quality of his spoken English became the talk of the town, and his schedule stayed constantly filled with tours. Therefore, he could soon have some choice as to which groups he guided.

SamSan loved his work and had never been happier. His new occupation proved to be more lucrative and less dangerous than importing durian could have ever been. Not only did he receive a two thousand riel monthly salary plus generous tips from his patrons, but most shop owners gave him a five percent commission on all items sold to the parties he brought to their businesses. He and Guek rented an apartment on the third floor of a relatively new, western-style brick building in an upscale neighborhood in Phnom Penh and began to live the good life.

He particularly liked to show the crocodile farms, most of which were run by Vietnamese residents of Cambodia. A majority of these farms were located in Area Four (four kilometers outside of Phnom Penh). Feeding the crocodiles made quite an exciting spectacle, especially for the children, and the adults treasured the specialty items made from the hides of crocodiles, such as handbags and billfolds. SamSan's parties could easily reach these farms by pedicab, a passenger-carrying rickshaw either pulled or pedaled by a human being. Some of these pedicabs bore ornate decorations, but they were more expensive to rent.

One particular Vietnamese crocodile farm became SamSan's favorite place to tour. Ong Sao (meaning "Sixth Son" in English) owned this farm, and he not only charged reasonable prices for his quality goods made from crocodile skins, he presented a good show with the feeding of his carnivorous creatures. Best of all, he gave SamSan a higher commission than the other crocodile farm owners offered. The pair soon became fast friends.

SamSan had guided tours at SOKHAR Voyages for less than three months when US Senator Mike Mansfield from Montana came to the agency for a tour. Although a member of the royal family had the official title as the senator's tour guide, he asked SamSan to show the Royal Palace and the Apsara. Senator Mansfield then boarded an aircraft that quickly whisked him away to Siem Riep for a tour of the famous Angkor Wat temple.

A few days later, the US Embassy in Phnom Penh reopened. That pleased SamSan greatly, and he said to Guek, "Senator Mansfield's visit is probably the reason the embassy has reopened. I believe that Cambodia's relationship with the United States is finally warming up. Now perhaps the United States can help us get rid of those communist military bases that Prince Sihanouk has allowed to operate openly here for such a long time."

SamSan often disagreed with Prince Sihanouk's policies, but that did not prevent his friendship with the ruler's nephew, Prince Pheanureak, from blossoming. The pair became inseparable and shared their innermost secrets.

One day Pheanureak said to SamSan, "You seem to be preoccupied or worried about something of late, my friend. What is wrong with you?"

"I am worried about Guek," SamSan confided in his friend. "She and I have been married for more than a year, and she has not become pregnant yet. Both of us are agreed that we want to have children, and I cannot help but wonder if something is wrong with one of us."

"I am afraid I cannot help you with that problem, my friend." Pheanureak laid a sympathetic hand on SamSan's shoulder and shook with laughter as he continued, "I have exactly the opposite problem. My wife seems to always be pregnant." SamSan then joined in Pheanureak's joviality as they shared a hearty laugh.

Political Upheaval

Under pressure from Washington, Prince Sihanouk changed his policy in 1969, and the Vietnamese Army bases were no longer welcome. President Nixon took the opportunity to launch a massive, secret bombing campaign called Operation Menu against their sanctuaries along the Cambodia/Vietnam border. About the same time, the Cambodian monarch discerned that the political winds were shifting, and he took an extended trip to visit France, Russia and China. He left Lon Nol, the prime minister, in charge of the Cambodian government in his absence.

Lon Nol shared SamSan's fear of a revolt from the 600,000 mistreated Vietnamese civilians in the country. He knew that they, along with the uncounted number of heavily armed Viet Cong and Vietnamese army troops located in those "secret" military bases throughout the country, could easily overcome the weak Cambodian Army. The prime minister hoped to quell that threat by leading Cambodia to closer ties with America and felt his best chance of achieving those ties was by stirring up large demonstrations against the Vietnamese presence in the country.

SamSan could not understand why Prince Sihanouk failed to return to Cambodia in the face of Lon Nol's actions. It was much later when he realized he should have suspected something was afoot. Sihanouk's son, Prince Yuvaneath, took fifty-one high-ranking officials and their families with him and left the country.

Buoyed by Prince Sihanouk's non-action, thousands of supporters of Lon Nol marched on the North Vietnamese Embassy in Phnom Penh on March 11, 1970, in vigorous protest of the Vietnamese presence in Cambodia. That same morning, SamSan hosted a party of eight Australians on a tour of Phnom Penh. As they passed by the embassy on their way to the royal palace, the leader of the Australians exclaimed, "My God, look at that crowd."

SamSan frowned as he saw a mixture of students, monks, and soldiers milling around the embassy grounds. Many of them carried anti-Vietnamese banners and heavy clubs. His fear index rose even higher when he saw smoke issuing from the embassy building.

"Let's go and see what is happening at the embassy," said the Australian leader.

"I would rather not," SamSan objected. "I cannot be responsible for what might happen to your party if I let you go into a mob like that."

"But I need to get some pictures," the Aussie replied. "If something important is happening at that embassy, those pictures might be worth a lot of money when I get them back to Australia. Come on, mate, I say let's go."

In spite of SamSan's objections, the group bolted and ran into the middle of the demonstration with cameras flashing in all directions. As they dashed onto the embassy grounds, they headed toward the building's battered-down door. "We had better not go inside," SamSan pleaded. "Any situation becomes much more dangerous when you are inside a building."

"Oh, come on, mate. Don't be a spoilsport. This could possibly be the chance of a lifetime for me. I am going in there whether you come or not. These pictures may make me rich and famous back home," said the group leader as he headed for the embassy building, still frantically aiming his camera and snapping pictures of everything that was happening.

Inside the smoke-filled embassy building, the elbow-to-elbow crowd seemed to take delight in destroying anything and everything in sight. The crowd had literally torn the huge and heavy metal door to the embassy vault from its hinges, and it lay flat on the floor. Contents from the vault littered the entire room. Several bundles of American currency that the mob had attempted to burn were scattered on the floor. Since the money appeared to be there for the taking, SamSan succeeded in liberating two bundles of large bills worth about five thousand dollars.

"Thank You, God. It is almost as if You have given me a gift," he said as he finally exited the building along with his party. He felt a sense of gratitude for the safety of the group and for his financial good fortune as he concluded the tour. He and Guek threw quite a party that week, financed by the North Vietnamese government.

Lon Nol grabbed absolute power in a coup one week later. He immediately issued a decree that all Vietnamese must leave Cambodia within ten days. His order applied to both civilian and military Vietnamese. The order made no exceptions for those who held Cambodian citizenship or for those who had been in the country for many years. He promised that the Cambodian Army would guarantee safe transportation for each family to the common border between Cambodia and Vietnam. He also promised that the CIC (an international group that controlled the border) would oversee what he referred to as their "repatriation" from that border on to their destination in Vietnam.

When the government made this announcement, frantic Vietnamese business and property owners began frenzied efforts to convert holdings into gold or cash. Houses and businesses often sold for as little as one percent of their actual value. "I bought a rental house for only fifty dollars of my newfound American money," said SamSan.

Lon Nol also issued an executive order that no member of the royal family could leave Cambodia. He feared they might go to another country and set up a government-in-exile. Before Lon Nol's subordinates could implement the process to carry out this order, Prince Sihanouk succeeded in having his mother flown to Paris. However, SamSan's friends, Prince Pheanureak and Princess Danin, remained trapped in Phnom Penh. Pheanureak promptly moved to Battambang near his wife's family, and SamSan lost contact with his friend.

When these rapid-fire events took place, SamSan remarked to his fellow tour guides, "Prince Sihanouk is no longer in charge of the country, but he is giving his support to guerilla groups in remote areas, especially to the Khmer Rouge. They have really stepped up their activities and the Americans have started to bomb military targets in Cambodia. We are definitely at war, and we cannot expect to have any more tourists."

A Friend Is Murdered

Lon Nol extended the ten-day grace period for Vietnamese evacuation by fifteen days, but many of the civilians still failed to comply with his order. The Vietnamese Army and Viet Cong units that Prince Sihanouk had allowed safe haven for many years paid no attention at all to the order. They carried on business as usual in open defiance of Lon Nol's directive.

SamSan still went to work every day, but because there were no tourists, he had to draw heavily on his five-thousand-dollar "gift from God" to support his current lifestyle. After more than a month with no tourists, a New Zealand couple with one child finally came to SOKHAR Voyages for a tour. Lon Nol had already extended the grace period for Vietnamese to exit the country several times, and this was the absolute last day.

SamSan showed the family a few of the sights in the city, and they requested that he show them a crocodile farm. As the party neared Ong Sao's farm on the Mekong River, they looked on in horror when they stumbled on uniformed Cambodian soldiers looting anything of value in the area. SamSan tried to hide his fright from the couple as he said, "Something terrible is happening here, and we need to turn back right away."

As soon as he reached home, he borrowed a neighbor's motorcycle and returned to Ong Sao's farm to check on his friend. When he crossed the bridge to the deserted business, he came face-to-face with the sight of Ong Sao's dead body lying half-submerged in his crocodile pond. Only his head, with one eye hideously contorted, parts of his skeleton, and one foot, with its shoe in place, remained. Memories of his grave-robbing experience as a youth flashed through SamSan's mind, and he had the same response. He vomited.

"Oh my God," were the only words he could find to wail as he immediately turned the motorcycle around and hurried home. "It was horrible," he said to Guek. "I cannot imagine how any human being could be so cruel to another human … and all because he was Vietnamese."

Sleep refused to come to him at all that night, and the following day brought even more problems.

Genocide

Jacques Renault, a French citizen who had been only a casual acquaintance of SamSan, had flown his Vietnamese wife to the relative safety of Saigon. When he came back to Phnom Penh to transport the other members of her family to safety out of the country, he found their home ransacked and empty. Unable to find any indication as to where her family might have gone, he asked SamSan to help him in his search for them.

"You have been in this country for a long time and know this area quite well," SamSan said. "Why do you need me to help in your search?"

Jacques replied, "I may need you to translate for me if whoever has taken them does not speak French. I can understand the Khmer language fairly well, but my vocabulary is somewhat limited and I do not speak even the words I do know very well."

"What are you proposing that we do to try to find them?" SamSan asked the frightened Frenchman.

"I suppose the only choice we have is to go out Highway 1 toward the Vietnam border. If the government troops have taken them, perhaps we can catch up with their convoy before they get out of the country. Then we will see how much of a bribe it will take to get them back. I have rented a Mercedes 280-S we can use in the search. It will cover more ground than any other vehicles I know of, and it can do it in a hurry."

"How many people are in her family?"

"Let me see. There is her mama and papa, her grandmother, and six kids ranging from six years to eighteen."

"What will we do if we find them? There is certainly not enough room in a 280-S for nine of them and the two of us along with their belongings."

"To hell with their things," Jacques said in reply. "We will tie the kids on the roof of the car if we have to. It all depends on what the situation is when and if we find them, but we have to try something.

My wife would never forgive me if I did not make every effort, and I cannot think of anything else to do. Can you?"

SamSan shook his head and sadly admitted, "No, I cannot think of anything else—not under these circumstances."

The pair knew their search would take them into a region where civilian travel was restricted and someone might question their presence there. Therefore, the Frenchman put a Red Cross armband on his left arm to give him some appearance of legitimacy. SamSan wore his tour guide uniform that identified him as an employee of the Cambodian government and made his presence legal in most areas of Cambodia.

They followed Highway 1 as it wound along near the banks of the Mekong River and had traveled several kilometers before they spotted a convoy—a large bus and a number of Cambodian Army trucks—loaded with Vietnamese civilians. "Perhaps your wife's family is in that group," SamSan said.

"I hope and pray to God that they are," said Jacques. "About all we can do right now is to follow them and pray for the best."

"Keep enough distance between them and us so it is not obvious that we are following them," SamSan warned.

The convoy moved along at a slow pace until, surprisingly, it stopped in an uninhabited area where the highway came very close to the river. "Why are they stopping at this godforsaken place?" Jacques wondered aloud. "It is several kilometers short of the border with Vietnam."

"Perhaps this is where the CIC will do their inspection and take over the convoy to carry the people on into Vietnam," SamSan suggested. "If that is the case, it should be a good place for us to show ourselves and try to get them back."

SamSan and Jacques pulled their car into the bushes so they could watch for an opportunity to approach the convoy and look for Jacque's kinfolk. They could hardly believe their eyes when they witnessed the soldiers forcing the unarmed civilians from the vehicles.

They made every one of them place their valuables in a common pile. The soldiers took a few of the prettier young girls to a location far removed from the larger group. The remaining Vietnamese— male and female, adult and child—were killed by the soldiers, some with a rifle shot to the head, some thrust through with bayonets. The lifeless bodies of the victims were then thrown into the Mekong River until it ran red with their blood for about a hundred meters.

When a young soldier, who appeared dazed by this gruesome assignment, wandered close to their vantage point, SamSan dared to step out and question him. He assumed that his uniform would give him an official look to one so young.

"Why are you doing such a horrible thing?" he asked the trembling soldier.

"Our commanding officer says we need exercises like this to show that we have the nerve to kill human beings in combat," the soldier replied without blinking. "He says that because Prince Sihanouk always wanted Cambodia to be neutral, we younger soldiers have been without any kind of combat training. He thinks this will help us become combat ready in a hurry."

"What will happen to the young girls you separated from the group?" SamSan continued, fighting the nausea that was about to overwhelm him.

"They are the reward of our battalion commander for his diligent work in our combat training. We are supposed to take them to him," the young soldier replied.

"What is the name and number of your battalion, and who is your battalion commander?" SamSan asked in obvious anger.

"You had better leave before I report you to my commander," said the soldier as he made a threatening gesture with his rifle. "What outfit are you with anyhow? That is a strange-looking uniform you are wearing."

"I am with the official government of Cambodia, but that is not the question of the moment. Surely you realize you are slaughtering innocent civilians. Some of these people could even be your neighbors," said SamSan, who could hardly hold back the tears. In spite of this plea, the soldier simply turned away.

As he and Jacques drove back toward Phnom Penh, SamSan mused in absolute silence for a while. Eventually he spoke, "I never dreamed I would witness genocide by soldiers from my own country. It is too bad we did not have a camera to record that massacre. Now we have absolutely no proof of what happened, since they threw all of the evidence into the river.

"But I guess it really does not matter. We do not have a name or number for the battalion or the name of the battalion commander to make a report. Furthermore, I do not have a single contact that I know I can trust in this new government. Where could we possibly report it?

"Our only hope for your wife's family now is that they were not in that convoy and might have made it into Vietnam some other way. We must pray that they will get in touch with you soon."

Jacques simply shrugged.

"I see dark days ahead," SamSan said.

"What will I tell my wife?" Jacques muttered.

Meanwhile, the Khmer Rouge and other insurgent groups stepped up their activities in the rural areas of Cambodia, now that they had gained the political backing of Prince Sihanouk. A definite aura of war hung over the country of Cambodia.

A FIGHTER FOR FREEDOM
Military Service in Vietnam

Dong Bathin, Vietnam—Early 1971

One could not expect even the opulently wealthy royal family to
continue salary payments to tour guides who no longer had tours to
guide. SOKHAR Voyages, hoping for peace and calm to return, held
on to most of their employees for a few months before they assigned
SamSan and the other tour guides to a ragtag paramilitary group
called "The Commandos." The group received some rudimentary
army training from old veterans using outdated French army rifles
and antiquated equipment, mostly from the First World War.

In early 1971, SamSan transferred to the Cambodian Army and
received a commission as a second lieutenant. He reported to the
village of Dong Bathin near Cam Ranh Bay air base to undergo
interpreter training. He relished the idea of serving with the US
forces in Vietnam and his assignment to an American unit, the 51st
USARV Individual Training Battalion, but he missed Guek terribly.

After completing a twelve-week training course, he became the
interpreter for the personnel unit of the 324th Battalion of the First
Division, and met Maj. Jimmy Lee Osteen. When the major became
aware of the quality of SamSan's spoken English, he confided to the
young Cambodian, "We are terribly short of good interpreters in this
unit, and it hinders our training of Cambodian recruits every day. I have
been thinking that, with your background in language, you might have

some friends who would be interested in doing this kind of work. Is there any way you can help us recruit several more guys who understand and speak reasonably good English? They will not have to join the army. It will be a civilian job, and it pays a very good salary."

"I think I know several people who might be interested," SamSan replied, thinking of his out-of-work associates from SOKHAR Voyages.

Major Osteen recommended a promotion for SamSan to first lieutenant and dreamed up the impressive title of Chief Military Civilian Interpreter Recruiter for his new emissary. SamSan's chest swelled with pride over his new rank and assignment. The fact that he would be able to stay in his home and visit Guek on his trips back to Cambodia made things even better. Perhaps there was still some hope they could start a family.

Chief Military Civilian Interpreter Recruiter

Vietnam/Cambodia—Early 1971–73

He returned to Phnom Penh by the next available military aircraft and looked up his fellow former tour guides at SOKHAR Voyages, most of whom still had no employment. Over the next several days, he succeeded in recruiting nine civilian interpreters for the military. He secured transportation to Vietnam via C-123 transport for his new recruits and proudly accompanied them to his base. His infectious smile seemed even larger than usual as he happily herded his prizes to meet Major Osteen.

SamSan took frequent trips between Vietnam and Phnom Penh to recruit translators. This gave him the chance to enjoy some time with Guek and his friends. He returned to Vietnam each time victoriously bringing from one to three recruits. Between those recruiting trips, he filled in as interpreter for the American soldiers who were training Cambodian recruits in the Dong Bathin camp. He could not have been happier, but he learned that, despite his exalted opinion of them, not all Americans are perfect. Not all of them conformed to the same mold that formed his friends, the Allisons.

It was the middle of 1971, and he had been in the Dong Bathin camp for only a few months when a company of Viet Cong guerillas crept up on the fringes of the camp one night and began to launch rockets and fire rifles into the area of the camp that housed many of the Cambodian trainees. In the confusion caused by the attack, Major Osteen ordered SamSan to go to all three of the Cambodian Training battalions.

"Order the men to get down flat on the ground and stay low until this thing is over," he said. "They do not know how to defend themselves, yet."

As SamSan went through the area shouting his warning, he realized he was the only person in the area who remained standing, and yet no harm had come to him. This realization brought a certain smug feeling of indestructibility to him. Then, he saw the observation tower that rose above the latrine, and he climbed up its stairs to get a better view of the attackers. From this vantage point, he could clearly see the muzzle blasts in the pitch-black darkness and could easily spot the exact location of the attackers.

"Hand me that AR-15 rifle with the M-79 grenade launcher attached and get me some extra ammo for both of them," he said to the frightened latrine orderly. Then he began to return the fire of the creeping enemy singlehandedly.

When the burly American, Sergeant Lawrence, saw his highly valued interpreter being exposed to enemy fire, he bellowed, "Lieutenant Ouch, come down from there this very minute!"

"No no no. I must not come down. I can see exactly where their fire is coming from, and God is protecting me," SamSan responded to Sergeant Lawrence's order. "We are in a position where we must fight back. If we do not return their fire, they will come even closer. Then their rockets and rifles will be more effective and hurt more of our soldiers. I absolutely must not and I will not come down."

"Then I am coming up there with you," retorted Sergeant Lawrence as he grabbed a 60 mm machinegun and ran up the stairs. "Them slimy little SOBs ain't gonna shoot at me and my men and me not do anything about it," he muttered as bursts of fire from his machinegun began to pierce the darkness of the night.

For a few minutes that seemed like only a few seconds to the exhilarated SamSan, the sky was aglow with small arms fire traveling in both directions. A rocket from the Vietcong was occasionally interspersed. During the firefight, Sergeant Lawrence received a small flesh wound to the wall of his abdomen, but SamSan did not receive a single scratch.

US Chinook helicopters arrived shortly with their floodlights and M-60 machineguns. When they began to fire, that brought an abrupt end to the conflict, and SamSan returned to his quarters. The survey of the battle scene the following morning revealed seven or eight dead Viet Cong, and SamSan could not help but wonder if he were responsible for any of those deaths. The Cambodian trainees suffered the loss of six men plus a few minor flesh wounds. Everyone agreed the result would have been much worse had it not been for the brave actions of Lieutenant Ouch and First Sergeant Lawrence.

Because of his ability to speak several languages, SamSan occasionally served as a forward air observer for B-12 bombers while he was at Dong Bathin. In this role, he had to spot targets for a group of ten American bombers based at UTAPAO or Samak San, in Thailand. He could relay information from either South Vietnamese or Cambodian frontline units to the American airmen with considerable accuracy. For these critical missions, his assigned code name was "Hotel Soma," which his friends later shortened to simply "Soma." It was his first truly American nickname, and he would cherish that title for the rest of his military career.

A few months later, when his American commander gave his written evaluation of SamSan, it read:

> Lt. Ouch's superior and multiple linguistic abilities have been invaluable to us. He is a totally loyal soldier and can be depended on to carry out orders with efficiency and dispatch. When he is away from us on his translator recruiting duties, both the quality and the speed of our training of recruits diminish. The accuracy and effect of our air attacks improve noticeably when he is available to serve as a forward air observer and can use his superior translation skills to direct the B-52 pilots. He is quite observant and makes good tactical decisions. He has proved that he is fearless under enemy fire on more than one occasion.

Blood on His Hands

As he traveled back and forth between Vietnam and Cambodia performing his duties as a recruiter of translators, SamSan could not help but notice the bands of rogue Cambodian soldiers that roamed the streets of Phnom Penh. These soldiers, armed and in uniform, terrorized citizens throughout the city.

When merchants asked them to pay for services or merchandise, these derelicts often threatened shopkeepers with violence, and sometimes carried out the threat. They also took whatever they wanted from the general population and claimed it was for their army units. These overt acts of violence turned many people in the civilian population against the Cambodian Army. SamSan became concerned about that situation and the bad effect it had on citizen morale and on the Cambodian war effort. He tried several times to get the ear of his superior officers in Phnom Penh and have these soldiers arrested, but it was all to no avail.

On one of his visits home, Guek told him about the murder of a teenage Christian Chinese girl. "You remember Su Li," she said.

"She was that beautiful young girl who was such a talented leader of the young people in the church we sometimes go to here in Phnom Penh. She was walking home from school the other day, and a group of those awful soldiers kidnapped her. They took her to a deserted pagoda on the outskirts of town and held her for two days. They apparently drugged her and raped her many times. She was unconscious when they found her, and she died without ever regaining consciousness. Naturally, she could not identify her attackers."

A litany of memories of Christian persecution flooded SamSan's mind as he heard this report. He immediately relived the rocks and rotten tomatoes thrown at him as a child while he was sitting in church. Even stronger than that, he relived momentarily the catastrophic depression in his life when Rev. Allison and his family had been forced out of the country in 1961 by the hatred of many Cambodians for all Christians. Never before had he felt so much anger as the useless death of this promising young girl brought to him. A strong sense of obligation came along with that anger. He felt he must see this murder avenged.

He had been powerless to do anything about those evil events in the past, but now he had a few connections with people in high places and a small amount of rank and power of his own. He made a solemn vow to himself and to the spirit of Su Li that whoever had done this demonic deed would pay for it.

"Those evil and godless scoundrels will get what is coming to them," he said through his tightly pursed lips.

He gathered a group of military and civilian friends to investigate the case. The group soon developed strong leads and collected considerable evidence against a certain group of eight derelict soldiers. A number of witnesses had seen this group driving an A-2 military Jeep in the area of the pagoda about the time of the murder. As the evidence mounted, SamSan and his friends felt certain these were the ones guilty of the rape and murder. They took their evidence to Major Oliver at the U S embassy who, in turn, contacted Major Ty

Houn of the Cambodian Military Police. They turned over their evidence to the major and pressed charges against the soldiers. Local authorities took all eight suspects into custody.

When SamSan spotted the group of hoodlums on the street again scarcely a week later, his anger hit the ceiling.

"How did you get out of jail so quickly?" he asked the leader of the group.

"Our commanding officer went to MP Headquarters and told them he needed us to carry out our military duties. When he told them that, the authorities released us back to our army unit. After all, we are soldiers, and it is our solemn duty to fight for our country," the smug soldier answered sarcastically.

SamSan shook with rage as he said, "You murdered one of the finest young Christians I have ever known. I will see to it personally that you do not get away with it."

"Go ahead. Have us arrested again," the unrepentant soldier taunted. "We will be out of jail as soon as our company commander hears about it. As smart as you are, I am certain you are already aware that our company commander is kin to me. In fact, he is my cousin."

A few days later, SamSan was driving his Jeep down Monivong Boulevard in Phnom Penh when he spotted the group's ringleader hanging out near the theater. He rounded up two associates, and the trio confronted the outlaw. When SamSan unholstered his prized Smith & Wesson 38 caliber pistol he had traded for in Vietnam, the smug soldier offered no resistance and climbed quickly into the Jeep.

"The Christian watch-dogs have come to take me back to jail," he mocked. "Now I will get three free meals a day until my cousin comes to have me released."

However, SamSan did not head for the military police station as his prisoner expected. He drove to an isolated spot on the edge of Phnom Penh near U Dong Mountain. The trio forced their prisoner out of the Jeep and into a brush thicket about a hundred meters from the road. By this time, the soldier realized his severe predicament and began crying. "Please do not kill me."

SamSan's partners twisted their prisoner's arms behind his back to restrain him. Meanwhile, SamSan, shaking with anger and excitement, screamed at him, "Down on your knees, you dirty scumbag! Beg for your life like that little girl must have begged for hers."

SamSan wanted to force a confession out of the soldier before witnesses and then turn him over to the authorities. As he pressed the muzzle of the loaded pistol to the sobbing soldier's left temple, their captive fell to his knees and began to cry hysterically.

"Please, do not kill me. Please, do not kill me," he begged repeatedly through his tears.

"Why should there be any mercy for a devil like you when you showed absolutely no trace of mercy to that young girl you killed?" SamSan said as he pressed the gun even harder into his captive's temple.

Suddenly, the soldier jerked his left arm free and hit SamSan's elbow. The jolt caused the pistol to bark loudly, sending its bullet through the soldier's brain. His body began to convulse wildly, and he fell forward. He was dead before he hit the ground.

"God forgive me. I did not mean to kill him!" SamSan said in near hysteria. Then he asked his friends. "What should we do now?"

"We had better get away from here right this minute," one of them said in a near whisper. "That shot might have attracted someone's attention."

"And the sooner we leave, the better," said the other companion. "Leave the SOB lying exactly where he is. The Khmer Rouge will probably be the ones who get the blame for his death. It is common for them to kill a Cambodian soldier and leave him in this area. Do not worry about it for even one second, Soma. He deserved to die. I only wish I could have been the one who pulled the trigger to kill him."

Nevertheless, SamSan knew who had pulled the trigger, and he knew he would never again be the same. He had taken a man's life.

Even if he had not intended for the confrontation to turn out that way, he felt convicted.

A Gamble for Guek

In his many air flight hours spent traveling between Vietnam and Cambodia, SamSan intermingled with a large number of high-ranking officers of both the American and the Cambodian military. His most frequent travel companions were Colonel Amos and Lt. Colonel Jameson, the American military attaché and air attaché to Cambodia respectively. In fact, on every return trip to Vietnam, he required Colonel Jameson's signature authorizing transportation of the new interpreter recruits he escorted.

On one visit home in 1972, Guek snuggled up to him and said, "You know, I have never been on an airplane, and I have never set my foot outside of Cambodia. Why are you not willing to let me have an adventure and go to Vietnam with you just once? You take all those other people with you on those American planes. Why not me?

"I can stay with some of my distant relatives in Saigon, and it will not cost us anything. I can sell some of this jade we have to pay my expenses. It has just been lying around the house gathering dust ever since we have been married. We would never miss it at all. Please, darling, it would mean so much to me," she implored.

"But," SamSan responded, "the people I take with me are traveling for military purposes, and those are military airplanes we travel on. I cannot carry just anybody I want to take on a military airplane, especially not a civilian. If I got caught, they could court martial me, and I might end up in jail for a long time."

Guek answered him simply with tears and silence.

A few days later, SamSan handed a travel voucher that bore Guek's name to the transportation officer in charge of boarding the C-123 transport. He hoped this particular document looked exactly like every other travel voucher he had so often presented before. He tried to appear calm, but he sweated profusely until the voucher had been accepted and filed. His worry centered about Colonel Jameson's forged signature that he, not the colonel, had affixed at the bottom of the page. His worry was in vain.

Guek spent two weeks visiting distant relatives and seeing Saigon. She met several important people, including Major General Clelent, and General Abrams, the chief US Commander in Vietnam. She sold jade to pay her expenses and to buy several gifts for friends and relatives back home. In spite of his gnawing conscience about his deception, SamSan enjoyed the closer relationship with his wife that his risk-taking engendered for him on this trip to Saigon as well as on his frequent visits home. However, he promised himself never to make that deception again.

The war in Vietnam did not go well for SamSan's beloved American forces. When the United States signed the Paris Peace Accords on January 27, 1973, and American forces withdrew from Vietnam, he returned to Cambodia for reassignment in Phnom Penh. Reunited with Guek, his well-loved wife who had still not become pregnant after more than four years of marriage, he resigned himself to the thought, *I will never be a father.*

Military Service in Cambodia
The General's Aide

Phnom Penh, Cambodia—February 1973

Because of SamSan's unheard-of language capabilities and his extensive contacts with high-ranking American and Cambodian officers, General Ith Suong, commander of the First Cambodian Division, ordered that the young lieutenant serve as his personal assistant. The First Division had responsibility for all of the area surrounding Phnom Penh, with its main responsibility being the security of the Presidential Palace.

In his new assignment, SamSan answered to the pleasure of the general. His duties spanned a wide range—from running personal errands for the general to the hazardous combat duty of acting as a forward air-ground controller directing bombing action for B-52s. SamSan's assignment actually was to do whatever the general asked him to do.

He liked being back in Phnom Penh because he could live at home with Guek. He probably liked even more being near the national soccer stadium where the Cambodian Army soccer team practiced. He spent every minute he could snatch watching the team and making suggestions. The coaches and players were surprised at his knowledge of the game and his resourcefulness for obtaining donations of small supplies needed by the team. In short order, the team requested him to take the position as team business manager.

SamSan had been working with General Suong for only a few weeks when the general summoned his young aide into his personal office. "Soma," the general said, "I understand you have been helping our Cambodian Army soccer team and are something like a team manager for them. I also know that in your previous assignment of recruiting interpreters for the United States, there were many occasions where you had to arrange air transportation back and forth between Vietnam and Cambodia for those interpreters."

"That is correct, sir," SamSan responded.

"I suppose, then, that makes you the perfect person to contact the American air attaché and ask the American military to fly our soccer team to the Queen's Cup tournament in Bangkok," said General Suong.

"But, sir," SamSan pleaded, "Colonel Jameson is no longer the American air attaché. He has been replaced by someone I do not even know."

"Nevertheless, Lieutenant Ouch, you know the procedure for getting permission to use space in American military aircraft quite well. It will not be difficult for you to make contact with this new air attaché. After all, his office is right here in Phnom Penh. He is not in Washington, D.C., or New York.

"Here is the problem. These are difficult and perilous days, and the morale of our troops—in fact, the morale of the entire country—is quite low. I understand that our army soccer team is reasonably good this year, and they might win some games in the Queen's Cup. This might give our national morale a boost, so I want you to do what I said when I began this conversation: I want you to arrange air transportation to Bangkok so our Cambodian Army soccer team can represent our country in the tournament. There is not enough money in my treasury to finance such a trip, and we need to do this for the sake of the morale of our country."

"I will do the best I can, boss." SamSan used a very unmilitary, personal term for General Suong, whom he respected more than any other high-ranking officer in the entire Cambodian Army. He gave the general a wink as well as a snappy salute and left the office.

It was late in 1973 when SamSan walked into the office of Col. David Opfer, who had replaced Col. Jameson as air attaché and military adviser to the Cambodian Army. "Sir," he said as he gave his best salute to the ranking officer, "I am Lieutenant Ouch, SamSan, a special aide to General Ith Suong, but most of my American military friends call me Soma."

Before SamSan could give his reason for being there, Colonel Opfer smiled at him and said excitedly, "So you are this guy, Soma, that Jimmy Osteen and Bob Jameson have raved about. You absolutely will not believe some of the things I have heard about you. In fact, I cannot bring myself to believe most of them."

"Major Osteen and Colonel Jameson were my good friends, sir," SamSan responded shyly. "It almost broke my heart to see them leave Cambodia, though I am certain they did not share my feelings of sadness."

"They tell me you will do anything you can possibly do to help the war effort in Cambodia. In fact, they say you can do almost anything, and if you cannot do it yourself, they tell me you know someone who can arrange to get it done," continued Colonel Opfer.

"They are too kind and much too high in their assessment of me, sir," replied SamSan with a blush.

"It is strange—almost eerie—that you should walk into my office right at this moment," said the colonel. "I have your efficiency report on my desk even as we speak, and I have been looking at it today. I am looking for the right man to help me in the job my superiors have recently asked me to carry out. This report says you are fearless under fire, totally loyal and dependable, and can speak several languages.

"You will need all of that and more in the job that Major Osteen and Colonel Jameson have said you were the unique person to fill for me. I need an undercover agent to help me figure out who is stealing so much of the money and material America is supplying to the Cambodian Army."

SamSan's ashen face fully registered his astonishment, and he stammered, "Colonel Opfer, I am flattered that you have gotten good reports about me and that you would want me for this assignment. However, my present assignment is as personal aide to General Ith Suong, the commanding general of all Cambodian forces around Phnom Penh. He has sent me here on an entirely different mission.

"I will readily admit that the request from the general might sound trivial when compared to the serious situation you are speaking about. However, before I can give any answer to your request, I must present the general's request to you. Also, the general has to release me from my assignment in his office before I can make any other choices."

"So you are the right-hand man for old Ith Suong, are you?" Colonel Opfer said with a laugh. "Tell me, what does that sly scoundrel want that he could not have asked me about at the party we both attended last night?"

"Please, Colonel, do not refer to my general by names such as 'scoundrel.' In my opinion, the general is probably the finest officer in the entire Cambodian Army. I am proud to serve him," SamSan said.

"Way to go, Soma," said the Colonel. "You just proved one of the points my report makes about you. The report said you were totally loyal, and when I called your boss something as innocuous as a 'scoundrel,' you immediately jumped to defend him. I like that. Now what is this secret mission your general Suong has sent you to ask me to do for him?"

"Sir," SamSan began, "I am manager for the Cambodian Army soccer team, and we have a very good team this year. Thailand has invited all of the Southeast Asian countries to play in the Queen's Cup tournament in Bangkok next June and the King's Cup tournament in November. These tournaments celebrate the birthdays of the Queen and the King of Thailand. Our team stands a good chance of winning some games and possibly even winning one of those tournaments this year.

"With all the advances the Khmer Rouge have made recently, the morale of the Cambodian Army and of the entire country is at an all-time low. The general thought a good showing by the soccer team might give a great boost to the morale of the Cambodian Army and of the country in general, but we have no money to get the team to Bangkok. The general hoped you might find a way to transport the team to Bangkok in one of your C-130 aircraft."

"What?" Colonel Opfer shouted. "Here in the middle of a war for the very existence of your country, he wants me to take an airplane away from delivering supplies for your soldiers and use it to carry some other soldiers to play games? I have never heard such a harebrained idea."

"But, sir," SamSan's voice sounded desperate, "the general is thinking of the morale of Cambodian soldiers everywhere. I know that most of your planes are empty when they return to Thailand. It should not be a real problem to get us there with so many planes flying empty when they go back to Thailand, and we could come back on a one-by-one basis, whenever there is a spot open in a plane coming to Cambodia. You would not have to miss delivering one piece of equipment for the war, and the general could try his plan to do something about our army's morale. The way I see it, it would basically not cost you a thing, and it could possibly make a huge difference for the Cambodian Army and the country."

Colonel Opfer grinned and said, "You have already got this thing figured out, haven't you, Soma. Those guys told me you were resourceful. I guess I should not have been surprised that you had an answer ready. That is exactly what I need in this job I am talking about having you to fill—someone who is intelligent and resourceful and who speaks this language and understands this culture. The more I see of you, the more I am convinced you are my man.

"By the way, how many people are on the Cambodian Army soccer team?"

"Approximately thirty-five or forty, sir, when you count the managers, trainers, and other ancillary people," SamSan replied.

"I'll tell you what, Soma; you tell old Ith Suong I will make the deal with him if he will release you to work for me right away. Tell him I will get his team as a unit to Bangkok for the games in June and in November—but they will have to come back to Phnom Penh on a space available basis.

"How long will you be gone?"

"About six weeks, sir ..."

"Six weeks?" the colonel exploded again. "My God, man, we could fight a whole military campaign in six weeks. Why should anything like a soccer tournament take so long?"

"Well, sir," SamSan explained, "We need at least two weeks on location to get ready for the tournament, and the tournament itself lasts for four weeks. All the countries in Southeast Asia will be represented, and Cambodia cannot afford to take a back seat at a critical time like this."

"I suppose you are right, Soma. It might look bad politically for them not to show. I am not much at this politics stuff. I am more of a military man," Colonel Opfer said in agreement.

"Now, about this job I have for you. It is very dangerous, and you are not required to take it. If you do take it, and we are successful and not too late in starting it, we might possibly be able to turn the tide of this war.

"On the other hand, if we are unsuccessful, Cambodia is certain to fall. How about it, Soma, can I count on you?"

SamSan's deep bow and slight smile did not hide the quiver in his voice as he said, "Sir, both Cambodia and America are fighting for freedom. My life would be a small price to pay for that. If the general will release me, I will consider it an honor and privilege to help in any way I can."

A New Team

"Soma, your efficiency report tells me you are very observant," a stern Colonel Opfer said to SamSan at their initial meeting as a team. "You will certainly need to use that trait if we are to track down the money and materials that are disappearing from the American aid to Cambodia. Tell me what you have seen among the officers and men of the Cambodian army that could explain that disappearance."

SamSan gave a low whistle and nervously squirmed in his seat. Colonel Opfer stared for a moment at his young Cambodian associate with a look so penetrating, it made him feel even more uncomfortable. Then the colonel continued his quest for the needed information. "I know it is not your nature to be a whistleblower, Soma, but when the security—and even the freedom—of your country might be at stake, it is high time for you to take tough action. I will ask you the question one more time. What have you seen in your observations of the Cambodian Army that would explain the disappearance of so much of the money and materials from the American aid packages?"

SamSan briefly cast his eyes on the floor before looking Colonel Opfer directly in the eye and giving a very short answer. "Cambodians, sir."

Colonel Opfer tried to suppress a small grin at this surprise answer. Then he continued to press for a more specific answer to the lingering problems that plagued Cambodia in this near dismal situation. "And what is that smart answer intended to mean, Lieutenant Ouch?"

"Sir, it is not a smart answer. It is a truthful answer," SamSan responded. "Ever since I began to notice things as a small boy, I have seen my countrymen far too often be guilty of graft and corruption. Officials have always been subject to bribes, and Cambodians have bought position or favor, including myself on one sad occasion when I needed Cambodian citizenship to continue my education. That self-serving attitude and practice has carried over into the Cambodian Army, and it continues to be prevalent in our government, too.

"Prince Sihanouk always wanted Cambodia to be a neutral country, so he did not care about having a strong army. His military leaders did not have much military education or experience, if they had any. Those leaders are the ones who are still in major control of the military forces, and the army suffers for it. Many of the very high-ranking officers have bought their positions, or perhaps they received them because of their family's social prominence. Some of them have absolutely no interest in the military, and yet they are supposed to lead our soldiers in battle—"

"Okay, Soma," Colonel Opfer interrupted, "that may explain why their tactics are so poor, but it does not explain what is happening to our money and materials—"

"But, sir," SamSan interrupted the colonel, "I am not through making my point, and you have some involvement in the story I was about to tell."

"Then go ahead, Soma," said Colonel Opfer with his interest obviously piqued. "By all means, tell me this story that involves me."

"Sir, it has to do with Neak Luong."

"Neak Luong?" Colonel Opfer erupted, "What the hell do you know about Neak Luong that I do not already know? I caught literal hell about that place."

"I know you did, sir." SamSan smiled sympathetically. "And I also know that you were simply caught in the middle of that embarrassing situation. If you believe Sidney Schanberg and Dith Pran's stories in the *New York Times*, Neak Luong was practically wiped off the map because of a US pilot error. It is true that there was a great deal of damage and quite a few casualties in Neak Luong, but my informants tell me that US pilot error was not the cause of the problem. They tell me it was an intentional plot by the Khmer Rouge to play up to the anti-war protesters in America and to discredit America before the world. My sources say that the Khmer Rouge paid a forward air observer in the Cambodian army to give the wrong bombing coordinates to the American pilots.

"Colonel Opfer, as you know, I am a trained forward air observer, and I have a considerable amount of experience with American pilots. I have never known the US bombers to miss a target. They hit exactly where we told them to hit every time in my experience. The Khmer Rouge knew if they could make the United States produce a large number of civilian casualties, it would add to the agitation of the anti-war demonstrators in the United States and drive more Cambodian citizens to become Khmer Rouge sympathizers. My informants say that particular forward air observer defected to the Khmer Rouge shortly after his traitorous act, but they did not trust him. I am told they quickly turned on him and killed him."

Colonel Opfer leaned forward and asked expectantly, "Who was the SOB, Soma?"

"I have never been able to find out his name, sir," SamSan replied. "Cambodian Army records are so unreliable that I do not believe we will ever know."

"Well," Colonel Opfer said, "that is a new wrinkle on that situation for me, but it is too late for the information to do us any good now. If the Khmer Rouge did outsmart us there, it is water over the dam."

"I understand that, sir, but I thought it might help your feelings about Neak Luong, and it would illustrate how subject to bribes my people are," SamSan added. "That self-serving tendency spills over into other areas and makes you have to be constantly on guard about money and materials."

"That tendency may explain why it is happening, Soma, but it does not explain who is doing it or how. I am sure you have heard the six-point formula for any investigation. You need to know who, what, when, where, why, and how. As we begin, we know what is happening; things are disappearing. We know it is happening all over the country and it is happening now, and it is because of greed. The two things we do not know are how it is happening and who is doing it. That is what you and I will investigate, and we had damn well better find out quickly and do something before your country falls.

"Tell me, Soma, who do you think is stealing the money and materials, and how do you think they are doing it?"

"I cannot answer that question at this time, sir," responded SamSan. "I have not been in the field with Cambodian Army units enough to actually observe how equipment and money are handled. As you know, most of my time has been spent recruiting interpreters or working as an interpreter for American advisers or as a forward air observer—but I will tell you what I am hearing. I am told that much of the cash money is siphoned off at the highest levels by generals and colonels, but I have no way to know who is doing that or how it is done."

"Yeah," the colonel said as he stroked his chin in deep thought. "I can see how a first lieutenant would have problems trying to check on his generals and colonels. That will have to be my job. Tell me, what do you know about the disappearance of those things at the lower levels, and how can we find out about that?"

"I do not know anything personally, sir, but my informants say there is a huge black market in military weapons and explosives everywhere. I hear these are stolen from Cambodian Army supply rooms and sold to crooked businessmen who then sell them to the Khmer Rouge at enormous profits," SamSan answered.

"That market appears to involve small amounts of weapons and explosives in each sale, but it is so widespread, it drags down our strength. I am told this kind of black market activity is more common among battalion-level and lower, commissioned and non-commissioned officers. I do not know how the soldiers make those shady deals, but I am certain we can follow those trails pretty easily."

"I am sure you are right about that, Soma," said Colonel Opfer. "A Jeep or an artillery piece has to leave some kind of track somewhere."

"When you speak about the money," SamSan continued, "I have also heard that most of the money that disappears at lower levels is siphoned off by battalion and lower level paymasters in the form of salaries. Those officers also keep a lot of the money intended for their troops in their pockets. Based on what I have heard, that is where our greatest military problem lies."

"How is that, Soma?" Colonel Opfer sat upright.

"A battalion is supposed to have between four hundred and five hundred men to be at combat-ready strength," SamSan continued. "They tell me that sometimes when a Cambodian battalion is engaged in a battle, it might lose, let us say, a hundred men to injury, death, or desertion. Then, the battalion commander does not report the loss, and he pockets the salaries of a hundred men at the next pay period.

"When that unit goes back into battle, the troops are fighting with their numbers reduced. Add to that the fact they are sometimes fighting against their own stolen weapons and following leaders who have no military knowledge, you can see why we have lost so many battles to smaller, less well-equipped Khmer Rouge units. That is a big part of the reason why the Khmer Rouge is making so much headway of late."

"I can see how that is happening, but tell me another thing, Soma," said Colonel Opfer. "Why do the Cambodian people allow Khmer Rouge soldiers to live among them, and yet they do not embrace your own government's forces? The Khmer Rouge are fighting against your way of life, and the Cambodian Army is fighting for it. It does not make sense."

"I believe there are two reasons for that, sir," replied SamSan. "The first and biggest reason is fear. The Khmer Rouge are ruthless and will kill anyone in a heartbeat who stands in the way of their mission. They seem to have absolutely no fear of dying for their cause.

"We have just discussed the second reason—the theft of soldiers' salaries by Cambodian Army officers," SamSan said through clenched teeth. "Those officers sometimes tell their troops the US government did not send the money for their pay, when the money is actually already in their own pockets or already spent. That lie not only makes the soldiers mad and they feel they cannot trust the United States, but they have no way to support their families. Then they take things from civilians at gunpoint. That, in turn, makes the people angry and the cycle keeps on going.

"On the other hand," SamSan added, "the Khmer Rouge troops get solid support from China and Vietnam, and their leaders are unselfish in fighting for their cause. Their troops' families' needs are met by those funds and, therefore, it goes back to the graft and corruption problem we are trying to tackle now. These scoundrels line their pockets at the cost of Cambodian lives and without any regard for the liberty of the Cambodian people. I would love the chance to stop some of that thievery and make those criminals pay for what they have done to my country."

Displaying a huge smile, the young Cambodian continued, "Sir, when and where do we start?"

"Well, first of all, we need more specific information and a plan of attack," said Colonel Opfer. "Perhaps we can use your connection with the Cambodian Army soccer team as a cover for some of your investigative work while we gather this information and come up with a plan. I will ask General Suong to give you a temporary duty assignment as the soccer team manager while they are getting ready for the Queens Cup. That will give you a lot of free time and a reason to associate with men from quite a few different military organizations. It will also give you a reason to visit any Cambodian Army unit in the country, supposedly trying to find soccer players for the army team. And who knows? You might uncover some jewels. This assignment should be the perfect cover for you in this operation. What do you think?"

"It sounds great to me," SamSan responded. "I cannot think of two things I would rather do than help my country's soccer team and try to stop the corruption that is ruining my country's army. I ask you again, sir. When do we start?"

The Investigator

As Colonel Opfer and SamSan studied the tactical situation they faced, they decided on a first mission that required a different kind of cover for SamSan. The soccer team connection would not work for him in an area controlled by the enemy and with no Cambodian Army garrison. For this operation, he would pose as a businessman and go into Kro Kur, a small village under Khmer Rouge influence, about seventy kilometers southeast of Phnom Penh, an area well known for black-market activity. The investigators felt it might be easier to pick up the players in this black-market game at the end of the trail where they made the sale, rather than in their home territory where the thefts occurred.

The plan seemed quite simple. By purchasing a small amount of sugar on the black market, he hoped to get evidence of the source of supply of illicit sugar that flowed into Phnom Penh from this small village and of any connection it had to the military. More importantly, he could keep his eyes open for any black-market activity in small arms and ammunition in that area. Colonel Opfer had given him five thousand riels to use for buying sugar "for his small family store."

SamSan tried to hide his apprehension as he boarded the SEAATCO (Southeast Asian Air Transportation Company) aircraft bound for Kro Kur. The pilot, Captain Jimmy Jacks, showed no evidence of recognizing the rookie investigator and gave him no more than a perfunctory greeting. Jacks was the husband of Princess Danin and one of SamSan's closest friends. The flight had been booked under an assumed name, and he hoped this lack of recognition was an indication that his disguise was truly effective.

In this Khmer Rouge-infested area, his life might well depend on the effectiveness of his disguise. Wearing a business suit, sunglasses, and a stylish straw hat and carrying a *don rek* (a curved stick that could be placed across the shoulders and used for carrying heavy loads), he even felt like a businessman.

When the plane landed, the stifling humidity and heat that occurred between afternoon showers in the rainy season were worthy adversaries for SamSan as he trekked the four kilometers from the airfield into the village. As he wiped sweat from his brow and checked into his rented room, he mentally reviewed the plan Colonel Opfer had laid out for him—*find the source of the black-market sugar and see if its purchase or sale has anything to do with the disappearance of weapons. Also, document any other illegal activity that you observe.*

He had visited Kro Kur many years before and had some vague familiarity with its layout. Rumor had it that the town served as a direct pathway for sugar from the fields in Vietnam, through the jungles of Vietnam and Cambodia and into Kro Kur. From there, it was shipped into the larger cities. His informants said the Khmer Rouge used sugar to barter with local merchants throughout the country for stolen weapons and military supplies that Cambodian soldiers had sold to the merchants. The merchants then sold the sugar at exorbitant prices in large cities such as Phnom Penh.

On the morning after his arrival in Kro Kur, SamSan tried to keep his profile low as he puttered about from shop to shop in the village. He asked a few trivial questions and bought a few trivial objects. As he tried to size up the situation, he carried on small talk about merchandising with various shopkeepers. He asked in each place about buying sugar for his small family store, but not one merchant in the village admitted to having any knowledge of anyone who had even a small amount of sugar for sale.

About the middle of the afternoon, his pulse quickened as he saw a heavily loaded Cambodian Army Jeep pull to a halt and its driver, Major Danh from the 15th brigade of the Cambodian Army, emerge from the vehicle. SamSan had known Major Danh when they were both in basic training at Dong Bathin camp. He had thought little of Danh at that time; he thought even less of him now. Trying hard to appear nonchalant, he watched intently as the major headed directly for the office of the village director. When the door to the office closed, SamSan moved and sat on a bench just outside of the director's office so he could hear a major portion of their conversation. He had listened from that same bench earlier in the day and had gleaned nothing.

"What do you have for me this time, Danh?" asked the village director.

"I have some really good stuff today," the major replied. "There is a 60 mm machine gun, three M-79 grenade launchers, an M-2 carbine, two M-16 rifles, a couple of AR-15s, and about a hundred hand grenades."

"I might have some interest in your merchandise if you do not try to rob me," said the village official. "All of you 'salesmen' think I am making a huge profit from the secondhand garbage you bring me."

"Are you still paying the same lousy prices? This load I brought today ought to be worth at least twice as much as the measly pittance you usually give me," Major Danh complained. "You do not have any idea what I have to go through to get this stuff in the first place."

"You are paid well enough, Danh," replied the village director.

The major continued his grumbling. "And to get it through from Phnom Penh with all the roads being controlled by the Khmer Rouge is almost impossible. I am the one who is risking my life, and you make all the money."

The village director sent four men to unload the contraband from the major's Jeep and fill his vehicle with sugar until its springs began to sink. "As long as you bring us quality merchandise at fair prices, you will get through," he said. "Try to cross us and ... "

Major Danh appeared to get the unspoken message.

SamSan could hardly hide his excitement. He made his way back to another shop on the thoroughfare. "I have been told a man could buy a little bit of sugar here in Kro Kur. I need a few kilos for the small store my family operates in Phnom Penh," he said to the shopkeeper.

"I do not know anything about a place to buy sugar here," said the storekeeper testily. "I have not seen any sugar in Kro Kur since the war started."

SamSan simply smiled and left the store. His eyes made a thorough search of the area around the village director's office before he headed in that direction. By this time, Major Danh had left to return to Phnom Penh. As he entered the village director's door, SamSan flashed his roll of bills and casually mentioned needing "a small amount of sugar for my small family store." A few minutes later, he left that office carrying 20 kilos of sugar suspended from his don rek. The following morning, he breathed a sigh of relief when Jimmy Jacks still showed no sign of recognizing him as he boarded the plane for the return trip to Phnom Penh.

SamSan said in his brief report to Colonel Opfer, "Now we know at least a small part of the 'who' and the 'how' of our disappearing supplies."

When his report resulted in the arrest of Major Danh, the happy investigator said, "That is at least one of those scoundrels we will not have to worry about for a while." However, among the officers in the Cambodian Army, the search for the snitch had already begun.

Back in Phnom Penh, SamSan began to diligently pursue his mission of visiting the scattered Cambodian military units. He found his cover of trying to recruit soccer players for the Cambodian Army soccer team worked well. Most units allowed him total access to their records and to their personnel, which made looking for evidence of corruption or graft among the officers much less difficult. Although he did locate several very good soccer players as he made his rounds through a number of Cambodian army camps, he unfortunately did not discover a single star who could seriously better his beloved Cambodian Army soccer team.

However, the young investigator found several battalions that were significantly below full strength, even though their official report showed no shortage of personnel. When he compared the names on their roster to their official report made to headquarters, the discrepancy showed. He reported these units to Colonel Opfer. The colonel then arranged for another investigator to run an official inspection of the records of these units and keep an unofficial eye on the activities of their commanding officers in order to divert attention from SamSan.

Most of those units whose rosters were only slightly below the expected level had made honest mistakes and righted their records a few days later when an inspector pointed out the errors. However, there were some battalions who were a hundred or more men short. The commanders of these units had to answer before a court-martial—and the hunt for the snitch grew more intense.

A Purple Heart

On September 14, 1973, SamSan and Guek were busily planning to celebrate his 28th birthday the following day when Colonel Opfer called his chief investigator into his office.

"Soma," he said somberly, "I want you to make a trip to Kom Pot City for me. I need you to coordinate an airdrop of supplies to some Cambodian Army units that are having a hard time with the Khmer Rouge forces there."

"Colonel, I would normally be happy to do that, but tomorrow is my birthday, and Guek has already bought a whole lot of chicken and other foods. She has invited several people to a party at our house to celebrate. We want you and your wife to come too. I will be glad to go any time after tomorrow," SamSan replied.

"After tomorrow, hell," the irate Colonel said. "After tomorrow, our troops are liable to be wiped off of the face of the earth. I want you to go right now—this morning. Your birthday party is a matter of having a good time. Those supplies are a matter of life and death for those poor devils at Kom Pot City."

"Since you put it that way, Colonel Opfer," SamSan said, "I guess I am on my way to Kom Pot City. However, I hope you will do me the favor of calling my wife to let her know what has happened. I am not certain she would accept any type of excuse if it came from me.

She has her heart set on having a big party for me, but if you tell her this is necessary to save lives, I believe she will understand, especially if you and your wife will attend."

"Okay, Soma, I will tell the little lady for you, and we will try to attend your party," the colonel promised, "but they are waiting for you right now. You get out to the airport right away. I have already called Major O'Connell, and he will meet you there with a helicopter. Time is of the essence. Many lives may depend on those guys getting supplies right away."

SamSan did not even wait to change his clothes. He grabbed the already packed suitcase he kept in his office in the embassy building for such emergencies and hurried to the Colonel's waiting Jeep.

Major O'Connell had the helicopter motors running and ready for takeoff as soon as SamSan darted from Colonel Opfer's Jeep and climbed aboard. As they neared Kom Pot City after about a thirty-minute flight, they came upon a fierce battle raging with intense smoke rising from the rocket and small arms fire, as well as from the forests and buildings that appeared to be burning everywhere.

"Jesus Christ," said Major O'Connell, "Jesus Christ, I never saw anything like this before. Everywhere you look, it looks like a Fourth of July fireworks display."

"Colonel Opfer said the fighting was really intense, but I never dreamed it would be this rough," said SamSan. "Where do you plan to land, Major? I cannot even see the airfield."

"I have been in touch with the radio at the airport, and they tell me the best place would be the high school soccer field," Major O'Connell said. "That is where I am heading right now."

As the helicopter cleared the center of town and came to the high school, SamSan could see the dim outline of the soccer field. Major O'Connell deftly set the helicopter down in the center of the field and said, "You do not need me here anymore. Jesus Christ, I have done my job, and I am getting out of this godforsaken place. Jesus Christ, how am I supposed to see to fly out from here in all this smoke?"

An A-2 military Jeep hurried SamSan to division headquarters, where the young lieutenant felt a strong sense of being *persona non grata* with the commanding officer, Lt. Col. Prak Vannarith. This lack of welcome was not what he had expected—he certainly had not asked to come. After all, it was his birthday and his wife would be mad at him.

Against his will, he had come on a mission of mercy to act as a forward air observer in a mission called "Easter Bunny." His purpose was to try to help save Lt. Col. Vannarith's troops from annihilation. He would coordinate a delicate airdrop over the next few days to resupply the severely embattled division of the Cambodian Army with food, medicine, and ammunition, and he would do his job to the best of his ability whether Lt. Col. Vannarith welcomed him or not.

The first day of the resupply effort went well. Under SamSan's direction, the "Easter Bunny" mission had resupplied the central battalion. The next morning, he spoke with two other forward observers about what targets should be priorities for the drop that day by the C-130s. They were unaware that the old building they stood near served as an ammo dump for Cambodian troops and would be a prime target for the Khmer Rouge artillery.

Suddenly, an incoming rocket shrieked its warning, and the trio hit the ground just as the rocket made a direct hit on the ammo dump. The blast was literally deafening, and SamSan felt the sting of flying debris before he lapsed into unconsciousness.

When he awoke, his world seemed to be screaming, his ears rang so loudly—yet that screaming was completely devoid of intelligible sound. Both of his ears were bleeding, and they throbbed constantly. Blood trickled from his right elbow and his left hand, both of which stung like bees. When he struggled dizzily to his feet to check on his companions, he discovered that both of them were dead. The man on his right lay disemboweled, while the one on his left had suffered a fatal head injury. Except for his hearing—which the medic said would never again be normal—his wounds seemed minor. After removing a small piece of shrapnel from his right elbow, the medic sutured the wound, dressed the cut on his right hand, and returned him to his regular duty.

SamSan continued to function effectively as a forward air observer despite his temporary near-deafness and a splitting headache. It took almost four days before the resupplied Cambodian unit finally succeeded in repelling the Khmer Rouge attack and he could return to division headquarters and Lt. Col. Vannarith. In spite of the fact that everyone knew it was because of the resupply effort that the unit had survived this massive attack, the feeling of his being unwanted there still hung heavy in the air.

When "Operation Easter Bunny" ended, SamSan had no immediate transportation back to Phnom Penh. This lack of transportation delayed his return to Phnom Penh long enough for him to learn the reason for the pitiful plight of the Cambodian Army units in the area. Only one regiment stood in defense of the area, where there should have been three. Furthermore, he found that one of the battalions in that regiment could muster only one hundred sixty-seven men, and a second had only two hundred fifty soldiers as far as he could determine. The third battalion had its full complement of between four hundred and five hundred men when the battle began and had been almost solely responsible for the victory over the Khmer Rouge.

He also found considerable evidence that officers in the unit had illegally used large quantities of American-supplied rice designated for their troops to feed themselves and their families, or they had sold it on the black-market. They had received American military payment certificates, which were designed only for use by American troops in Vietnam, in payment for the contraband. That finding mystified the young investigator because the military payment certificates were easy to trace.

By the time SamSan returned to Phnom Penh, the sutured wound on his right elbow had become red and swollen, and there was a red streak going up his arm well above his elbow. During the days of

"Easter Bunny," the young lieutenant had been unable to take proper care of his wound. Fearing he had "blood poisoning," the military doctor ordered his admission to the military hospital in Phnom Penh.

He was shocked and angry when the hospital's male nurses demanded that he pay a bribe for the daily dressings his physicians had ordered. When they refused to change his dressings until he had forked over two thousand riel (about four dollars, American), he personally experienced the same type of financial graft he had viewed in so many military installations throughout the country of Cambodia. He was eager to get out of the hospital as quickly as possible, so he paid the nurses' demands for each one of his daily dressing changes.

Upon his release from the hospital, he made no report of the graft he had uncovered there. He definitely considered the possibility of making such a report, but he reasoned that the amounts of the graft were trivial when he compared them to most he had seen. More importantly, that report would certainly point the finger of identification directly at him. This could possibly expose his undercover activities and make him ineffective as an investigating officer.

Then "the cure might well be worse than the disease," as my doctor once said, he thought silently.

Soon after SamSan's release from the hospital, he learned that the military had arrested Prak Vannarith, the battalion commander in Kom Pot City. The colonel was charged with the theft of more than two hundred bags of rice and an undetermined amount of money found missing from his treasury, and SamSan feared that the search for the snitch had narrowed even more.

THE QUEEN'S CUP
Bangkok, Thailand—Mid-1974

As time for the fourth annual Queen's Cup soccer tournament grew closer, SamSan asked General Ith Suong to turn over his passenger list for the trip to Bangkok. His low whistle of surprise at seeing seventy-six names on the manifest instead of the forty or so he had expected caused the general to comment, "Well, you cannot expect us to have a team appear in something as important as the Queen's Cup without any supporters or news reporters. My wife would never let me go unless she could be with me, and she would not dare travel anywhere without our family. And then, there are the local dignitaries that must be catered to and recognized."

SamSan could not afford to be too critical of the addition of family members by the general, because he had already included his sister, Marilyn, on his manifest. He had listed her team position as "housemaid." For the past several years, Marilyn had been in a difficult relationship with her husband. Their marriage had been fine in its early years, but her husband used her continued clinging to her Christian heritage as an excuse to become abusive. Marilyn had indicated that she needed to get out of the country and had even hinted that she might divorce her husband and stay in Thailand.

To SamSan's great surprise, when he presented the manifest to Colonel Opfer, the colonel signed it without any changes or any question and cleared the soccer team and all guests for the trip. In late June 1974, the group boarded an otherwise-empty US Air Force C-130 for the flight to Thailand.

Bangkok, Thailand—Mid-1974

As soon as the team arrived in Bangkok, SamSan feverishly busied himself with getting everything ready for the all-important tournament. Three days later, he had completed every aspect of his preparation for his team's participation, and he had a few days of free time on his hands.

Not even the monsoon season could dampen the spring he felt in his heart as he boarded the train for a four-hour trip to Aranyaprathet, a resort town known internationally as a gambling resort that is located on the Thai border with Cambodia. However, SamSan had an entirely different reason for his journey. From Aranyaprathet, he took a pedicab to the tiny village of Wat Tana and knocked on the door of a small, well-maintained residence. No one could have prepared him for the reaction of the matron of the house when she opened the front door to her home.

By pure maternal instinct, Hong Diep recognized SamSan immediately as her son. Her face turned ashen white, and she immediately dropped to her knees. "Please forgive me for what I did to you, my son," she said as she plaintively held both hands together under her chin in a gesture of prayerful penance. "I have never been able to forgive myself. In spite of how things might have looked, I really did love you. I thought you were dying."

SamSan reached out his hands, gently pulled his mother to her feet, and wrapped both arms around her. "Mother," he said, "please do not do this to yourself or to me. I was dying, and you could not have done anything thing more about it. I honestly believe that if you had kept me, I could not have lived. You did exactly what you had to do under those circumstances, and it turned out to be the best for both of us.

"I know you loved me," he continued. "My adoptive mother, your friend, Su Ho, has told me about that so many times. You kept me and loved me for more than a year, counting the nine months I spent in your womb. Then, when it looked like I would die in spite of every effort you tried to make, you did the only thing you knew to do. You honestly thought it would be best for both of us—and it was, because God had it planned that way. He took care of the rest of the situation.

"I still have a great love for you in my heart. That is why I am here. Please try to let bygones be bygones. This is a happy time. Do not spoil our short time together with words of regret and with tears."

When the rest of his family learned that SamSan had come to pay a visit, they killed a young water buffalo and prepared a big feast in celebration. After meeting his half-sister, four half-brothers, and their families, he learned that the family had successfully operated a sawmill business for several years and that his stepfather, Saing Dinh, had died from a stroke slightly more than two years earlier.

During the waking hours of SamSan's visit, his mother clung to him almost constantly and begged him, "Let me go to the Thai authorities and register you as my son. That way, you will become a citizen of Thailand and will not have to go back to Cambodia and fight in that awful war. You are still recovering from the wounds you got in Kom Pot City, and your hearing is bad. You should not be a fighting man—you are too talented for that. Please do not go back."

SamSan tried to be gentle as he reminded her, "Mother, it is my duty to go back and defend my country. I have a responsibility to my government. They have entrusted me with a commission in their army, which I am duty bound to carry out. Please, Mother, relax and enjoy the short time we have together."

In the three memorable days spent with his family in Thailand, he filled in some facts about his birth that Su Ho could only speculate about. In addition, he realized a lifetime goal by becoming acquainted with that part of his family.

When he returned to Bangkok from Aranyaprathet, SamSan found an urgent message waiting for him at his hotel room. It said he should call the manager of the Thai soccer team. He immediately found a pay telephone and dialed the number listed on the note. The voice on the telephone said, "Lieutenant Ouch, this call has nothing to do with soccer. I want to give you an opportunity to earn more money than you will make in several years as a soldier."

"I have always been interested in making extra money," SamSan's tone was questioning, "but what would you expect me to do to make so much of it?"

"It will be the easiest five thousand dollars American you ever made, and all you have to do is carry a small package with you when you return to Phnom Penh. You will be paid half of the money when you pick up the package and the rest when you deliver it to my party in Phnom Penh," responded his Thai counterpart.

"It should be very simple since you will be traveling on a US military aircraft. The DEA agents hardly ever do checks on the people who travel with the military, but they are very thorough in their checking of a large percentage of people who travel on any commercial aircraft."

"What would I be carrying?" SamSan asked, feigning some interest.

"What would you suppose?" the answer to his question came as a question.

"I suppose it would be some type of drugs—either heroin or opium," SamSan said.

"Only I would really know," his recruiter replied. "You do not need to know."

"How would I carry this package?" SamSan asked.

"We will give you a special ornamental scarf, and it will be sewed into that scarf," said the conspirator. "It is so cleverly done, no one will ever notice it if you do not try to wear it with your military uniform."

"Give me a couple of days to think about it," SamSan replied, "and I will get back to you."

SamSan immediately called Colonel Opfer and told him of the situation. "What should I do?" he asked.

"Call the DEA offices in Bangkok," Colonel Opfer said. "Let them tell you what to do. I will be in touch with them to coordinate things from this end—but do be careful, Soma. You are dealing with some dangerous people here. We cannot have anything happen to you. Your work here is very important."

When SamSan asked the DEA officer what to do about the conspiratorial offer, he said, "By all means, take him up on it, Lieutenant. We will watch you constantly while you are here and see if we cannot find out who is your contact in Bangkok other than the soccer team manager.

"By the way, do not be surprised if you are arrested when you get home. It will be a part of the plan, but I will assure you that you will not be held long. Oh yes, and there will never be any consequences to your military career, because nothing about this will ever be placed on your record. It is strictly a deal between you and the DEA."

SamSan then called Colonel Opfer again and told him about the DEA officer's plan. "Should I go through with it?" he asked.

"You had better be careful, Soma," said the colonel. "These folks put no value on human life, and you could be hurt or killed. On the other hand, we need to help the DEA clean up some of this dope smuggling that is ruining so many lives. At the same time, we also need to continue with our work. It is as important as anything else that is going on in Southeast Asia at this time.

"Give me the name of this DEA agent, and I will contact him. If you do not hear anything from me in two days, go ahead with his plan."

A DEA Agent

Two days later, SamSan called his new partner in crime and said, "Tell me a little more about this plan. How much risk is there, and what would happen to me if I should get caught?"

"Oh, there is hardly any risk at all," his contact said. "A high percentage of the Cambodian soldiers that come here on leave are carrying for us when they go home, and I only remember one who was caught. He only spent a couple of days in the stockade, and then they released him. Do not even think about it."

"Well," said SamSan, "I have never done anything like this before, and I cannot help but worry. What do I have to do to get ready?"

"Not one thing other than telling me your waist size. Then go about your business as usual," his informant said. "Try to give me a bit of warning before you leave, and I will take care of everything else. We will deliver the merchandize to you in a surprising fashion shortly before you board the plane to go home. If you act normally, there should be no problem.

"But right now, it is time for the Queen's Cup games to begin. Good luck to your team, that is, until the time when your team plays mine."

The Cambodian Army team beat Malaysia by a score of 3–2 in their first game, and SamSan was thrilled. When the team from Laos beat his Cambodians by an identical score in the second game, he was equally disappointed. Now that it was time to go home, he wondered what would be the "surprising fashion" by which his contraband would be delivered to him.

He did not have to wait long. As he exited the stadium after his team's loss, a jolting collision with a person dressed as a Buddhist monk shook his entire body, and he felt a package shoved into his hands. By the time he regained his composure and tried to locate the delivery person, the orange hooded figure had melted into the crowd. *So that is how they deliver their merchandise*, he thought, and he wondered if the DEA had been watching.

SamSan now turned his attention to arranging transportation for the soccer team and their guests who must return to Cambodia on a space available basis. Of course, General Ith Suong, his family, and their guests had to be the first ones accommodated. After this came the city officials with their families and guests and the few members of the press. Next to board were the lower grade officers and, finally, the members of the soccer team.

As others in the party were boarding the airplane for the trip home, Marilyn approached her brother and said solemnly, "I am not going back to Cambodia with you. I have taken all of the beatings I can tolerate from that no-good husband of mine. Tell Mom and Dad I will send for the girls as soon as I get enough money. I have signed to be a housemaid for a family in Bangkok for at least a year, so you did not lie about my classification when you listed me as a housemaid on the docket with your colonel. Please tell my family how much I love them."

When the last Queen's Cup visitor and player had boarded an airplane for Cambodia, SamSan finally began his return flight home. Dressed in civilian clothes and wearing his special scarf around his waist, he warily took his seat, not knowing what would be the next event in this drug drama.

As soon as the plane taxied to a halt in the Phnom Penh airport, a squad of Military Policemen boarded it and began searching every passenger and crewmember. They went through every piece of luggage for each person. When they patted down the waist-scarf SamSan wore, they confiscated it along with the $2500 advance money he had received for delivering the drugs. They threw him roughly to the floor and placed him in handcuffs. He was carted off to the police station and booked on charges of drug smuggling and placed in an isolation cell.

A short while later, the police whisked him away from that cell to a hotel room in Phnom Penh. It took a few hours for both the DEA and the military police to debrief him before they released him and returned him to his duty with Colonel Opfer. Although SamSan tried numerous times to gain some information from the DEA in Bangkok, he never learned the result of his brief career as a DEA agent.

Things Start to Unravel

When SamSan returned to Phnom Penh, he was truly saddened to find the plight of the Cambodian Army much worse than it had been a few short days ago when he left. The Khmer Rouge had made both territorial and psychological advances. He heard reports of an army unit near Kondoa Chrom that had stolen virtually all of the livestock and other farm products from the civilians of the area, leaving them destitute. The scoundrels sold much of this booty in Phnom Penh for great profits. Because of numerous incidents of this type, the civilian population had begun to reject all Cambodian Army units and to welcome the Khmer Rouge as they advanced on the way to Phnom Penh.

Colonel Opfer quickly sent SamSan to Kondoa Chrom to investigate the situation and try to appease the local citizens. It did not take him long to determine which Cambodian Army unit had done this. The Cambodian Army arrested its commanding officer on charges of theft and selling stolen property, but it was too late. The Khmer Rouge had gained the territory without firing a shot, further tightening the noose around the already endangered city of Phnom Penh.

A few days after his return to Phnom Penh, he learned that a Cambodian lieutenant had stolen a GMC military truck loaded with three hundred AR-15 and M-16 rifles and more than seventy M-79 grenade launchers, along with hundreds of hand grenades. SamSan carried false papers to hide his real identity as he followed the culprit to Battambang. He turned his evidence over to the local Cambodian commander, who arrested the thief as he tried to sell his contraband to a Chinese merchant. The soccer team manager returned to Phnom Penh barely in time to get his team ready for the King's Cup tournament.

"Soma," Colonel Opfer said as SamSan prepared to leave for Bangkok, "we do not have the luxury of time to give as much of it to this tournament as we gave to the Queen's Cup, because the military situation in Cambodia is so much worse. You will not have two weeks to prepare on their field this time. One day should be enough, and you must come back the very day your team is eliminated. I need you here and so does Cambodia.

"You must be very careful and keep a low profile while you are in Thailand. Remember, you got involved in a smuggling scheme the last time. Those folks will still be in business and they have long memories. They will not have forgotten that they lost five kilos of opium plus $2500 because of you. Be safe and come back here on the very first plane that leaves for Phnom Penh after the tournament. Let someone else arrange to get the others home."

"Yes, sir, Colonel Opfer, and thank you, sir," said the young lieutenant, who felt awed that his colonel and his country needed him.

The tournament did not go well for the Cambodian team. They played the powerhouse and eventual winner, Korea, in the first game and lost 4–0. SamSan boarded the first plane bound for Phnom Penh to hurry back to his duties, as Colonel Opfer had instructed.

When he returned from the King's Cup tournament, Captain Jimmy Jacks met him at the airport. "Soma, am I evermore glad to see you. I thought you were never coming back, and I really do need your help," said the frustrated and angry air captain as he greeted his good friend.

"I am glad to see you too, captain. And what is the problem that has you so upset?" SamSan said.

"I am really worried about the safety of Danin if she stays in Cambodia," the captain said. "She has already received several threats on her life because of her uncle, Prince Sihanouk, and some of the statements he has released to the press. I have been trying to get her cleared to leave, but the minister of the interior, this Major General Ek Preong, keeps on bringing up Lon Nol's executive order forbidding any member of the royal family to leave. Up until now, I have not been able to find any way to get around that order. I want you to help me get her out of the country.

"I have even offered him a bribe high enough for him to live out the rest of his life in Switzerland, and he is so afraid, he will not even talk about accepting it. You know the ropes around this town, and your boss, Colonel Opfer, is one of the most influential men in this country right now. I need you to come with me and speak to this jackass before I kill him," Jimmy Jacks concluded.

"Man," SamSan gave a low whistle as he replied, "that is a tough order. If money will not talk to the man, why in this world do you think I can?"

"Because you work for the right man, and you know the ropes. All the brass here in Cambodia are deathly afraid of Dave Opfer," said Jimmy Jacks. "They think he could pull the air support to the troops and the airlift of supplies, and Cambodia would fall tomorrow."

"They just might be right," SamSan said with a laugh, "but that does not give me any power. You know, I am only a first lieutenant. I just work for the man."

"It is called 'power by association,' Soma, and I have seen you use it in small ways many times before." Jimmy Jacks finally showed a small grin. "Now, I need you to use that power in a much larger way for your friends, Danin and me. It could save her life."

SamSan lowered his head and said, "Tell me, Captain, do you believe in prayer?" His penetrating question took Jimmy Jacks by surprise.

"Of course I do," he answered.

"Then you had better put it into practice all night tonight. We will go and see Ek Preong tomorrow, but I do not know if there is anything I can do."

Major General Ek Preong

When SamSan and Jimmy Jacks entered the Interior Minister's office the next morning, their reception was like the weather, cool and dry. An aura of anger seemed to hang over the room as Jimmy Jacks glared at the official, who returned the look in like fashion.

"What are you doing back here?" Ek Preong stared icily as he yelled at Captain Jacks. "I have told you over and over again in the past several days, there is no way I can allow your wife to leave the country. I am under direct orders from Premier Lon Nol that no member of the royal family leaves here, and there is nothing I can do about it."

SamSan had to restrain the airline captain physically as he attempted to climb across the desk and attack Ek Preong. "You sit right there in the chair," he commanded his friend. "Violence is not the answer to our problem, Captain Jacks. The general has his orders from higher up, and he is obligated to carry them out. Unless we can help him find a legal and diplomatic way around those orders, you already have your answer."

The interior minister turned to SamSan and continued his tirade, "And why are you here with him, Lieutenant Ouch? Do you think you can out-talk me with your silver tongue? You know, I am very much higher in army rank than you are. I am a major general, while you are only a first lieutenant. Did your all-powerful Colonel Opfer send you here to tell me I had better let her go?" he shouted with his face red and his neck veins distended.

"As a matter of fact, sir, he did," said SamSan meekly, telling the lie he had sworn he would not tell. "You do know he is also CIA," the young lieutenant added, further compounding the lie.

At this statement, the minister of the interior's face turned from red to an ashen white, and SamSan added the coup de gras. "He says that holding the princess in Cambodia against her will could cause a withdrawal of all American aid and that Cambodia would then be left to stand or fall on her own."

"Oh my god," Ek Preong responded as he turned to Jimmy Jacks, "I had no idea it was that serious. If that is the case, I suppose I have no choice but to sign the order. Where is that exit visa form?"

Pulling a pen from its holder and a form from its drawer, he scribbled his name on the proper line of the document and angrily thrust it back to Jimmy Jacks.

"We are most grateful for your help in this matter, sir," said SamSan as he bowed deeply. "And if you need someone to speak to Premier Lon Nol about your action in the princess's case, please let me know. I am certain my boss, Colonel Opfer, will be happy to testify in your defense."

"Get out of here right now!" yelled the minister of the interior. "Before I change my mind and have both of you thrown into jail...You and your bribe offers and your political pressure..."

Holding tightly to the order for Princess Danin's safe exit from Cambodia, the pair left the interior ministry office post haste. "Thanks, Soma." said the relieved Jimmy Jacks. "If it had not been for you, I would probably be in jail for murder now, and Danin would never get out of this hellhole."

"You Americans have a saying that says something like, 'You can catch more flies with honey than you can catch with vinegar.' Captain, I suggest that you learn to put that saying into practice. It is hard to use muscle against brute strength. My kung-fu instructor convinced me that strategy works much better than muscle every time," SamSan said with a grin. "I just hope Ek Preong and Colonel Opfer never get together and compare notes about the things I said."

Jimmy Jacks wasted no time in getting Danin safely out of the country. He made a solemn vow to himself that as soon as he returned to resume his SEAATCO flight schedule, he would find a suitable way to repay SamSan for his invaluable help in obtaining her release.

Alone and Arrested

When SamSan reported for work the following morning, Colonel Opfer called him into his private office and told him, "Soma, I received word from Washington yesterday that they will be reassigning me to duty in the United States about a week from now. I had expected I would be here for at least another six months, but there is a military protocol problem in the American plans right now. I have a higher rank than the man they plan to send as a replacement for the chief US military liaison officer with the Cambodian government. That difference in rank would be against proper military protocol. Therefore, I will be going home six months early."

"Oh no, not right now." SamSan gasped and staggered almost as if a physical blow had struck him. "We were just getting to the place where our work might make a difference for Cambodia. Forget about the military protocol—if Cambodia ever needed you, she needs you at a time like this. What will be done about the investigative work we have been doing?"

"My replacement will have access to all of my records. I suppose he will be the one to continue the work, if it is done at all," replied a somber Colonel Opfer. "On a personal note, Soma, I would advise you to seriously consider the idea of taking Guek and joining your birth mother in Thailand. In my opinion, things look very grave for your country at this moment."

SamSan stood unable to look at his commanding officer for a moment. Then he said, "I agree with you completely, sir. I also believe that your leaving may well be the death knell for both me and my country. I thought we were beginning to slow their stealing down a little bit, but now there will be no one to chase them down. Those scoundrels can steal to their heart's content, and to hell with Cambodia…" SamSan wiped his eyes.

Gaining control of his emotions, he changed the subject. "Sir, I will look into our leaving the country right away if you think it is best for Guek and me and if you believe there is nothing more we can do for Cambodia."

"I believe it would be best for both of you if you left right away, my friend," Colonel Opfer said gently.

SamSan simply stood with his head down, either unwilling or unable to look Colonel Opfer in the eye. For one of the few times in a life that had been founded on and driven by words, he found no words that seemed adequate for this situation. He also found it very difficult to restrain the tears.

"Please do not take my leaving so hard, Soma," Colonel Opfer said as he observed the quiver of SamSan's lips. "It is not as if either you or I are going to be dead. Both of us should be happy because I am going home. However, it does seem sad having to leave you and Cambodia at a time when she is so vulnerable and when we might have been beginning to turn the tide a bit to help her. But, as the French say, '*C'est la guerre.*'"

On Wednesday evening, November 6, 1974, at the farewell party held for the Colonel and his wife, SamSan saw no reason at all for any gaiety. He and Guek said their tearful good-byes to his friend and boss as the last persons to leave the party.

His sleep that night proved sparse and fitful. The following morning, he reported for work much earlier than usual. His plans were to tie up some loose ends on one of his previous investigations before he and Guek left the country. SamSan had barely completed his report and placed it in a top-secret file only he and Colonel Opfer could access, when someone suddenly kicked in the door to his office and five or six bullets whizzed by his ears. He immediately sought cover by ducking under his metal desk.

"Stop your shooting. Stop your shooting!" he shouted. "I am not armed and I will not make any resistance. Just do not kill me."

He relaxed a bit when he heard the "cease fire" command that finally came from the captain in charge of the office invaders, a person unknown to SamSan. "Lieutenant Ouch," the officer ordered, "come out from under that desk this instant. You are under arrest."

"And exactly what charges am I facing and from what person do the charges arise?" SamSan asked as he stood with his hands held high.

"The entry on this warrant says you are charged with, 'heroin smuggling and treason.' I am afraid it says absolutely nothing about who made the charges," said the arresting officer, showing no trace of emotion.

One of the soldiers struck SamSan with his fist and rudely pushed him down onto the floor and put him in handcuffs. The arresting detail marched their prisoner at prodding bayonet point past the gawking line of clerks in the military office building to the waiting MP vehicle. Then they transported him to a large prison in Phnom Penh, only a stone's throw from Colonel Opfer's office. SamSan was booked on false charges of treason against the government of Cambodia and heroin smuggling.

Imprisoned
Phnom Penh, Cambodia— January 1975

Prison guards stripped away all of SamSan's identification and forced him to put on prison garb. The only personal items they allowed him to keep were his comb, and a small crucifix Guek had given him. His haughty keepers then pushed him rudely into a dimly lit, 2½ x 3 meter cell furnished with only a built-in cot. That cot had to function as his chair as well as his bed. An open drain in the floor served as his bathroom. Vulgar prison graffiti almost completely covered the grossly mildewed walls of his drab, dungeon-like cell.

During daylight hours, a bit of sunlight managed to trickle between the heavy bars guarding the ½ x 1 meter window, located very high on the wall to deter any effort to escape. Because of the window's height, he could see only the sky as he gazed through it. There were no trees or flowers within his vista. The only thing that could divert his attention from his pitiful plight was the sound of outside activity. They allowed him to shower three times a week, and this was the only time he ever left his cell.

The guards served his meals on a thin, tin tray shoved through a small slot in his metal cell door twice a day. Leathery GI-issue powdered eggs that SamSan thought should have been used to recap tires dominated the morning meal almost every day. Fortunately, they served a small amount of rice with the eggs, which made the meal slightly more palatable. The usual fare in the evenings consisted of *lo bok* (Asian turnips) and rice. SamSan hated lo bok in any form it could be prepared. He reasoned that the lo bok served in this prison doubled as an instrument of torture and should have been banned by the Geneva Convention. It was the worst he had ever tasted.

At first, SamSan was not particularly worried about his imprisonment. He had composed a letter to General Suong, his former boss, immediately after his arrest, telling him about the situation he faced and asking him for help. He had always felt he could count on the general to help him in any time of trouble. After all, even after the general had agreed to SamSan's assignment to Colonel Opfer, he had frequently called on his former aide to do something for him personally, to take a message to someone or to look after some family matter for him. Surely the general would have needed some small favor by this time and had learned of his imprisonment. The boss would not let him down.

When he had heard nothing from General Suong by the end of the first week, he was sorely disappointed and a bit frightened. A prison guard had promised to deliver the letter to the general, but it had to go through proper military channels. SamSan had no other choice but to entrust the letter to the guard, but now he wondered, *Has my letter been impounded? Where is the general, now that his aide-de-camp truly needs him, and why does he not contact me in prison? Better still, why does he not come and have me released?*

"God, please send the general or somebody else to get me out of this place," he prayed.

SamSan read the same ancient magazines over and over again. He looked at the same obscene graffiti on the same peeling and mildewed prison walls until he thought he would lose his mind, which almost constantly turned to Guek. *Why has she not come? Is she safe? What is she doing and who is looking after her? Does she know the dangerous situation I face? How could I possibly let her know?*

"God, please look after my wife for me. I cannot even look after myself right now," he prayed.

Bored almost to tears by inactivity, he longed for the action of the former days. Never had he experienced a time when he had absolutely nothing to do but think. *Could there possibly be a worse torture than to have thoughts and not be able to translate them into action? Now that Colonel Opfer and I are both out of their way, who will investigate the illegal—and sometimes even treasonous—actions of so many of the Cambodian military commanders?*

Colonel Opfer had assured SamSan that his country would fall if the two of them failed to weed out much of the corruption that existed in the Cambodian Army. His imprisonment undoubtedly stood as towering evidence of their failure in that effort. The only recourse left for him was prayer. He could do no more. His prayer was constant and repeated as he asked God to look after Guek and his beloved Cambodia and to send someone to get him released from prison.

SamSan could not help but wonder why God had not answered his prayers for release. Had God forgotten him?

He had endured almost two miserable months in prison before Jimmy Jacks returned from relocating his wife to the United States. As soon as the air captain reached Phnom Penh, he hurried to visit SamSan's apartment to thank him for his help in getting Princess Danin out of the country. When he found the apartment empty and boarded up, Captain Jacks felt a sense of panic and guilt.

He sought out a neighbor, who excitedly told him. "SamSan, he be held in prison near Olympic Stadium. Guek, she try to see him, but guards, they treat her bad and not let her see him. She say she had big husband and wife talk to tell him. She say she write him every day, but letters they all come back. She say she scared very much and so she go back home to Battambang."

Jacks went to the prison immediately to see SamSan and try to get him released. The first words SamSan spoke as he glimpsed Jimmy Jacks were. "Have you seen Guek? Is she okay?"

"I have not actually seen Guek, but I believe she is okay," said the air captain. "As soon as I got home, I went by your place looking for you to thank you for helping me get Danin out of Cambodia. Your neighbor told me what had happened and where the jackals were holding you. That neighbor said Guek told her she had written you every day, but all of the letters came back. She said that when Guek tried to visit you, she became terribly frightened because the prison guards treated her so badly. When the guards turned her away and refused to let her see you, she packed up her things and went running back home to Battambang.

"That relieves my mind a little," said SamSan. "At least I know where she is and that she has tried to contact me. I am glad to know she is at home with her family. Someone can look after her there."

"Oh yes, the neighbor also mentioned something about Guek's telling her she had an important message to deliver to you." Jacks added. "Guek did not tell her what the message was about. She said it was 'big husband and wife talk.'"

"Big husband and wife talk? Hmmm." SamSan appeared to be in deep thought. "I wonder what special message could she have had for me."

"Don't you worry a minute more, Soma. You will soon be able to go to Battambang to check on Guek and find out everything that is going on. I will have you out of this place in no time at all, and money is no object. After what you have done for Danin and me, we owe you that much and more," he said. "There is no doubt in my mind that we will be able to have you out of this place in a hurry. I know you do not like to participate in bribery but, after all, this is Cambodia. In this country, every man and everything has its price.

"By the way, Danin sends you her love and her thanks for what you did. She said she loves it in America," Jimmy Jacks said glibly as he left to see the commander of the prison.

Captain Jacks came back in just a few minutes. He seemed frustrated, angry, and agitated. "Soma," he said, "can you believe that joker turned down a bribe of more than a million riels? When I made him the offer, his face got very red and he threatened to put me in jail. He screamed right in my ear, 'No amount of money could buy his release. The minister of the interior has a direct interest in this man's case. I am not going to put my neck in a noose by letting him go—not for any amount of money.' And that is a verbatim quote."

SamSan appeared puzzled as he said, "So Ek Preong is the guy—or at least one of the guys—behind my being here, is he? That makes sense. My guess is that there are several more people involved in putting me here. But we will have to wait until all the cards are played out at my trial to see who the culprits really are."

"It appears that way," said Jacks. "And the thing that makes me feel so bad is, it is probably because you made him lose face when you backed him into a corner and forced him into releasing Danin. I am truly sorry about that, my friend."

"Oh, it is not your fault, Captain," said SamSan. "What I am thinking is that Ek Preong is one of the big shots in the government who is getting a cut out of the American military aid money that some of the high-ranking Cambodian military commanders are stealing and we were investigating. He is certainly in the right position to get a cut, being both a major general in the army and the interior minister of Cambodia.

"The way I figure it, he might have thought Colonel Opfer and I were getting a bit too close on his trail and might catch up with him, and that could be the real reason he has it in for me so badly. If that is the case, then the thing with Danin would only be an excuse for charging me with treason. He probably got some kind of report from the DEA about my help in their case with the Thai soccer team manager to help manufacture his case. Remember, he specifically pointed out to us that he is 'a Major General' and I am 'only a First Lieutenant,'" he added scornfully.

"Do you know of anybody anywhere who might help you get out of this place?" Captain Jacks changed the subject. "I will be happy to contact them for you."

Then he added, "I make you a solemn promise, Soma. I will be making the rounds throughout this country, and everywhere I go I will be constantly looking for someone who can do something about getting you out of this hellhole."

"You might try to reach General Ith Suong. He might help me … and … oh, yes," SamSan added. "You could contact my brother for me. I do not think he has any kind of political clout or that he can get me out of here, but who knows? Anyway, I certainly would like to see him one more time."

"I will contact both of them right away," said Jimmy Jacks as he left the prison.

A few days later, SamSan's brother, Captain Ly Chong Ky, came to the prison for a visit. He tried to gain SamSan's release through military channels, but the prison commander stonewalled his efforts as thoroughly as he had blocked Jimmy Jack's attempts to free him. However, the two brothers had a great time of family reminiscing.

No word ever came from the general. *Ek Preong has probably tied his hands and will not allow him to help me,* SamSan thought.

A couple of weeks later, a Cambodian Army captain came to SamSan's prison cell and asked, "Are you Lieutenant Ouch SamSan?"

"I am, and who are you?" SamSan asked.

"It does not matter who I am, nor is it any of your business. My rank is higher than yours, and you must come with me," said the officer.

"And exactly where are we going?" SamSan retorted.

"I am not at liberty to tell you, and it is none of your business anyhow," replied the officer with a haughty air of great authority.

"And what if I refuse to go?" SamSan asked.

"You have no choice but to go," replied the officer. "If you try to refuse, and if it is necessary, you will be put in a straitjacket and physically carried to this appointment. I am under orders to deliver you at this hour to a Lieutenant Colonel Prak Vannarith, and I intend to carry out those orders."

As SamSan rose from his cot and stood by the officer ready to leave, he said, "I believe I know this colonel. I think the two of us had some dealings in Kom Pot City at an earlier time."

The party traveled to the airport in Phnom Penh, where his escort led SamSan to a waiting helicopter and forced him to get aboard. SamSan did not try to hide his surprise and disappointment on seeing his subordinate, Second Lieutenant Am Ton, seated next to Colonel Vannarith. Three guards carrying bayoneted AR-15 rifles guaranteed everyone's compliance with the Colonel's orders.

Am Ton had been an office assistant to SamSan in his investigations. He was in charge of storing the general records kept by SamSan and Colonel Opfer, but he did not keep the secret files known only to the pair. He gave a subdued and frightened salute to his former boss. SamSan easily sensed that Am Ton had not come by choice.

"So we meet again, Lieutenant Ouch," said Colonel Vannarith as SamSan boarded the American-supplied helicopter and a soldier handcuffed him to his seat. "But this time, the circumstances are quite different. I am the investigator, and you are the one who is being investigated." Then he turned to the pilot and gave the order to take off.

The noisy helicopter began its slow ascent with ever-increasing speed until it reached a height of about five hundred feet. Then it flew in wide circles over the small city of Kondoa Chrom. Prak Vannarith turned to Am Ton and yelled above the helicopter sounds, "What did you say about me in your report to the American, Colonel Opfer?"

"N-N-Nothing, sir, I-I-I had not ever seen you before this morning, sir, so I had n-n-nothing to report to the American c-c-colonel or anyone else, sir," the lieutenant stuttered in a loud, frightened voice.

"You *lie!*" Prak Vannarith screamed. "I have seen the records you filed in the office, but they are not complete. What did you tell Colonel Opfer, and where are the other records that you must have put on file somewhere?"

"Sir," Am Ton replied, seeming to have regained some composure, "I swear by the tomb of Buddha, I never saw any other records, and I never had any other records in my hands. I did not have the highest security clearance. If other records existed, they must have been above my security limit. I had no knowledge of them and no access to them, and I never touched them. All I ever did with any records was to place them in the files. I made it a habit not to read any files, and I certainly did not read any record concerning you."

"You infidel, you lie and then you swear to that lie by the tomb of the great Buddha. You do not deserve to live a minute longer!" the red-faced Prak Vannarith screamed. He then turned to the three guards and gave the order, "Put him overboard right now."

"Please do not kill me," begged Am Ton. " I have told you nothing but the truth. I did not have any information to give to Colonel Opfer, so I could not have told him anything about you. I simply filed the reports he and Lieutenant Ouch gave me. I put them in their proper place, but I never read any of them. I am innocent of harming you in any way. I have small children. Please, for the sake of my children, do not kill me."

"He is telling the truth," SamSan interjected. "All he did was to file the report I made to Colonel Opfer."

"Put the lying infidel overboard right now," Prak Vannarith repeated his order to the guards.

The three guards finally overcame the resistance put up by Lieutenant Am Ton and pushed the screaming Cambodian officer out of the helicopter to his death. SamSan could only watch this horrible chain of events as he sat shackled to his helicopter seat.

The colonel then turned his attention to SamSan. With a cynical smile and in a soft voice, he said, "So now, Lieutenant Ouch SamSan, you have seen what happens to those who dare to cross Prak Vannarith. Do you want to have the same fate as your Lieutenant Am Ton? Or will you tell me right now exactly what you reported to your mighty Colonel Opfer?"

SamSan's calm demeanor belied the rush he felt inside as he said mockingly, "Sir, what reason would I have for telling Colonel Opfer anything at all about you? Have you done something wrong?"

"You know very well what I am speaking about, Lieutenant!" the livid Prak Vannarith screamed. "It was right after your visit to my unit in Kom Pot City that I was arrested and charged with stealing money and rice from my troops. I am no fool. I can put two and two together."

"But Colonel," SamSan said calmly, "if you will remember, I helped your unit in the Easter Bunny supply airdrop. When a Khmer Rouge rocket hit our ammo dump in that operation, it wounded me and knocked me unconscious. The two men standing beside me died. How could you think I came there to investigate you when you know my real reason for coming to Kom Pot City? It was to save your troops by directing the drop of supplies to them. Your conscience may be hurting you for something you have done, but tell me, how could a wounded man carry out an investigation of the type you accuse me of doing?"

SamSan's statement enraged the colonel even further. "You insubordinate little bastard," he said through clenched teeth and with tightly clenched fists, "I am tempted to push you out of this helicopter and kill you myself."

"I do not believe Colonel Opfer would like it when he comes back and finds out what you have done," SamSan said in desperation.

"What did you say?" the Cambodian colonel asked, suddenly subdued.

"I said, 'I do not believe Colonel Opfer would like it when he comes back and finds out what you have done,'" SamSan repeated his imagined story very calmly.

"Are you telling me that he is coming back to Cambodia?" the now white-faced Prak Vannarith inquired.

"That is what Captain Jacks told me the other day when he visited me in jail. He said he met Colonel Opfer in Washington, D.C., and the colonel said he would be here in just a few days. I believe he should be here sometime the day after tomorrow," SamSan continued the lie.

"Hmm," Colonel Vannarith mused. "It seems to me I did hear that the American pilot had come to visit you recently. In that case, you might be telling the truth. Perhaps we had better get back to the base. It will be bad enough to face Colonel Opfer in my court martial hearing. I certainly do not want to face a man with that much power in a murder case." He turned to his pilot and gave the order, "Return to base."

As he returned to the prison, SamSan prayed silently, "Thank You, Lord, for forgiving the lie that saved my life. In fact, Lord, I am not so certain it was not You who gave me the lie in the first place. You continue to amaze me with the way You look after me, and I am grateful. Amen."

The Lion, the Tiger, and the Crocodile

SamSan sat in his dank, drab prison cell a few days later, still dazed from his harrowing experience in the helicopter. He felt confused and completely exhausted as he shivered from both the cold and great fear. Gunfire in the distance and an occasional explosion of a rocket in the area close to the prison served as grim reminders that the Khmer Rouge were on the outskirts of Phnom Penh and could capture the city at any moment. He had heard the guards saying that Khmer Rouge forces had cut off the road to the airport. This meant no more American supplies would be coming in to support the retreating Cambodian forces.

Most of the jailhouse talk he heard exalted the Khmer Rouge and their "glorious leaders and the wonderful Kampuchea they wanted to create—a classless, agrarian society without any religious activity allowed." It nauseated him. He had tasted the results of communism in his youth, and it had not been pleasant. He wanted to respond to the statements but used his better judgment and resisted the temptation to debate the issues at this time. He knew that would make him an even greater target for the Khmer Rouge when, and if, they took over Cambodia.

Increasingly worried about his own future and that of his beloved country, he toyed only momentarily with the paltry meal thrust at him through the slot in the door. "Lo bok again!" he shouted as he shoved the tray back toward the guard. "Why not fill my tray with swill from the garbage can? It would taste better than your blasted lo bok."

SamSan continued to pace back and forth in his tiny cell as the guard devoured the meal he had refused. His mind seemed to be unable to focus on any one subject as it raced incessantly: *Where is Guek? How is she? What is the "husband and wife" message she has for me? Does the general know where I am? What is keeping him from coming and having me released? Does Ek Preong have him stymied too? How soon will the Khmer Rouge get here? What will happen when they do?*

Then he prayed, "God, only You can help me now. I am strictly in Your hands."

"What day is it?" he asked the guard.

"It is April 12, 1975," the guard answered.

Major sounds came from the nearby American embassy. Its paper shredders hummed loudly as they worked overtime. Because his window was too high for him to see anything but the clear, blue sky, SamSan had to visualize what was happening outside only by the sounds he heard. He assumed they were destroying confidential documents that absolutely must not fall into the hands of the enemy. Even louder were the sounds of helicopters.

He could visualize what was happening by the sound of helicopter after helicopter rising up from Olympic Stadium, the national soccer field. He could picture each helicopter filled to capacity with embassy personnel and a few selected refugees that the US government evacuated to safety away from the area. His heart beat with sympathy for his people and for the guards as he heard the embassy guards having to turn away many people who had worked for the

Americans and now realized that their lives were at risk because of that association. It sounded as if the embassy was in full evacuation mode, and he could not hold back his tears.

It was over.

The vision he had would never come to pass. There would be no victorious Cambodia with a new government modeled after that of the United States, with all of the attendant freedoms. He and Colonel Opfer had been too late in starting to combat the greed and corruption in the Cambodian Army and, drained of so many resources, it appeared certain to fall. When the American Embassy building emitted absolutely no sound, there remained no question in his mind. It was over.

That night, only the gruff voices and scuffling boot heels of guards making rounds in the prison and the increasing sounds of war from outside broke the silence. Both sounds made him cringe even further with fear. He noted that the guards no longer wore their uniforms, and he thought, *They are ready to blend in with the civilian population.* He fingered the cherished crucifix Guek had given him as a good luck charm, and his mind wandered again. *I wonder if she is okay.*

Four nights later, as he pondered his own seemingly hopeless predicament, SamSan could not suppress the small grin that came over his face when his mind wandered back to his childhood and he thought about the story Mrs. Allison told in Sunday school one morning. He visualized the young man she had told them about who faced a seemingly hopeless situation.

"Once upon a time," she had said, "there was a young man who found himself in a situation where he faced a tiger in the tree, a lion on the land, and a crocodile in the creek. This left him with no avenue of escape. What could he do?" she had asked.

Then she had given the answer herself. "He could only pray to God and ask for His help."

Realizing he faced a similar situation, his tortured spirit screamed in silent prayer, "God, could my situation be any worse? There is no way I can escape from this locked cell, and any of these rockets could kill me if they hit this prison. On the other hand, if the Cambodian Army fights off this attack and holds Phnom Penh, they want to try me on those trumped-up charges, and I am doomed for death. In addition, if the Khmer Rouge take the city and find out who I really am—an educated man, a Cambodian Army officer who worked with Americans and a Christian to boot—they would kill me on the spot without a trial on any one of those charges. Only You can help me out of this mess."

He lay dejectedly on his ragged, torture-inflicting cot in the dank prison and dozed for a short while. The eerie sound of sheer silence woke him from his fitful sleep, and he listened intently. No loud voices of prison guards or sounds of their heavy boot heels scuffling through the prison corridor rang in his ears. No longer could he hear the rockets whiz overhead and explode nearby or even the sound of rifle fire. This could only mean one thing: Cambodia had fallen. The guards had deserted the prison and melted into the civilian population. The Khmer Rouge had won.

He shook the door to his prison cell violently, but it would not budge. The cowardly guards had left him trapped like a rat in a cage and cornered by the Khmer Rouge. There was no way for him to run from them. Tears filled his eyes as he again felt of the small crucifix Guek had given him, and his mind wandered to her side again. *I wonder if she is doing all right, and what was the message she had for me?*

"God, You will have to look after her while I am in this mess. For that matter, You will have to look after me also," he prayed. "There is nothing I can do—"

Before he could finish that train of thought, the sounds of heavier-than-usual boots and of many military commands shouted in loud but unfamiliar voices announced the arrival of the Khmer

Rouge forces. Their soldiers took over the prison and the city of Phnom Penh quite early in the morning of April 17, 1975.

Those evil monsters have me now, he thought. *I am glad Guek is not here with me. She would be so frightened. Thank God, they stripped me of every bit of identification when they arrested me. I do not have any papers on me that show who I am. Perhaps I can hide the facts about my life from them. They would kill me in a heartbeat if only they knew.*

When he heard the sounds of a Khmer Rouge soldier's boots approaching in the hallway and the rattle of keys turning in his cell door, he huddled hopelessly in the corner of his cell. He fully expected instant death by a blow to his head with a heavy instrument—the typical mode of execution by the Khmer Rouge—and he dared not look.

As he bowed his head in what he thought would be his final silent prayer, he was amazed and grateful to have that prayer answered by a single word. The Khmer Rouge soldier's loud and raspy voice simply said, "Go!"

Released—to What?

SamSan walked out of the prison in absolute amazement amidst the maze of Khmer Rouge soldiers firing their guns into the air in jubilant celebration. Civilians wandered aimlessly about the streets completely bewildered, most of them crying. Some shed tears of anguish, some shed tears of joy.

As he merged into the teeming crowd, the logic of all that had happened to him suddenly dawned on him. *The Khmer Rouge made the assumption that everyone the Cambodian government held in that prison was a Khmer Rouge sympathizer. That is why they let me go without any questions. If I had been at home or in my regular office, they would have killed me without any further thought. I am certain that is why God would not let any of the efforts to get me out of that place meet with success. He could not spare my life in any other way but by leaving me in prison. Thank You, God.*

His sense of relief was the only thing that exceeded his sense of bewilderment as he walked out of the prison. The fact that his only worldly possessions were the prison clothes on his back, his crucifix and the comb in his pocket seemed unimportant. He no longer had those multiple death sentences hanging over his head. He had somehow escaped "the lion on the land, the tiger in the tree, and the crocodile in the creek" that had threatened his life. Now, he had a possible chance to survive.

"Thank You, God; thank You, God," he silently exulted in constant repetition as he exited the prison and scurried through the milling masses toward his home. When he got near his apartment, he could see Khmer Rouge soldiers already breaking windows to enter the building, so he abandoned the idea of trying to reclaim any property.

Guek is not there, he reasoned, *and I had better not show myself either. Too many things in that apartment would identify me and undoubtedly sentence me to death if they connected me to them. I had better leave right now before one of my Khmer Rouge sympathizing neighbors recognizes me and points me out to them.*

In another time, he might have mourned the loss of all of the personal items in his home, but he had his life and at least some measure of freedom. Those two items were far too precious for him to jeopardize them by trying to reclaim things. All he really needed was his freedom and to be reunited with his wife. He had one of these now, and he felt certain he would soon claim the other.

He wrestled with the question about where he should go at that moment. The obvious answer was to Battambang to search for Guek, but he had no supplies for such a trip, and he had no money to buy those supplies. Therefore, he headed back to the city and the anonymity of its milling crowd. That should give him a little time to think.

As he picked his way through the pressing crowd, he formulated his plan to stay alive: *Under no circumstance can I allow them to know I am a Christian or a Cambodian Army officer or that I worked with*

Americans. They must not know that I have an education and can speak other languages. I will speak only when spoken to, and I will only use the broken Khmer that most uneducated Chinese in Cambodia speak. I will claim to be a simple seller of noodles. There will be no more Ouch SamSan, because I will go by my childhood nickname of Ly Peing. I must get rid of this crucifix, but I will pray to God and thank Him for every day I survive.

Back in the center of town, the Khmer Rouge soldiers were in nearly as much disarray as the local citizens, and they showed as much confusion. There seemed to be no organization to any of their movements, and no one appeared to be in control. Soldiers ran here and there, smashing windows and taking the spoils of war, civilian and military alike.

The Cambodian Army had simply vanished by donning civilian clothes and melting into the citizenry. Many American-made military vehicles lined the streets in the area, abandoned—but only a very small percentage of the Khmer Rouge soldiers knew how to drive them.

As SamSan started to walk past him, a Khmer Rouge soldier pressed the muzzle of a rifle ominously into his side and grabbed his shirt. "You there in prison clothes, can you drive one truck?" he demanded.

"Y-yes, me can drive one truck," he mumbled in broken Khmer, bowing and feigning great ignorance.

"How you learn to drive? You one of them rich folks?" the soldier demanded as he pressed the bayonet on his rifle against SamSan's side.

SamSan feigned a huge smile and bowed low again as he told, for the first time, the lie he would tell many times in the future. "No, no, me sell noodles, but boss, he had one truck. He teach me drive."

"Then, you will teach us drive," said the soldier as he released SamSan from his grip and showed a trace of a smile. He handed a key to SamSan and led him to a nearby truck.

"You wait here," said the soldier, and he disappeared into the crowd.

The "Death March"
Phnom Penh, Cambodia—
April 17, 1975

SamSan sat in his newly assigned truck and watched in stunned silence. He saw history in the making as total chaos continued to reign in the city of Phnom Penh. Wave after wave of conquering Khmer Rouge troops continued to pour into the city, many of them firing their rifles into the air in a show of triumph, all of them shouting and cheering. Hundreds of thousands of citizens greeted the conquering troops with true joy in their hearts that the fighting and death had finally come to an end, but many of them still harbored deep regrets at the loss of a comfortable way of life.

As if the confusion produced by an incoming occupation army with the rowdy actions of the victorious troops were not enough for the city, the Khmer Rouge political leaders compounded the confusion very shortly after their arrival. The frantic scream of their loudspeakers began to saturate the air. They overpowered all other noises in the city with the ear-piercing, false jeremiad they repeated over and over and over again, "The United States Air Force will begin bombing this city at any minute. All citizens must evacuate Phnom Penh immediately. You must leave the city by the numbered highway nearest your home. This is a temporary evacuation and will last for only a few days, so do not try to take any possessions with you. Angkar will look after your belongings in your temporary absence, and we will keep them safe and secure, waiting for you to return to your homes in safety.

"All people must leave—young and old, sick and well—there will be no exceptions. You must leave the city immediately before the bombing begins. You must travel at least four kilometers beyond the city's edge before you attempt to stop. This will make it easier for Angkar soldiers to clear the town of any pockets of resistance that might come from remaining decadent Cambodian army troops and will not endanger the citizens of Phnom Penh. It is for your own protection that we demand that you do this. You do not wish to die at the hands of the dirty Americans and their bombs."

Under normal, peacetime conditions, Phnom Penh had boasted a population of approximately six hundred thousand people. However, that count had swelled to possibly as much as two million people because of the huge number of refugees who had sought the protection they believed America would afford them in their capitol city. Now every one of these permanent residents, as well as all of the refugees, had to leave the city. Many of them reacted in sheer panic on being forced out of their homes and into the streets.

A few people trusted the Khmer Rouge to keep their word and look after their belongings. They left everything behind as they evacuated the city. However, the sight of Khmer Rouge soldiers already openly looting businesses and homes belied their loud promise of safekeeping for valuables. Therefore, most of the citizens made an effort to carry everything they valued as they made their hasty retreat from the city.

People pressed their automobiles, ox carts, two-wheeled push-carts, wheelbarrows, bicycles, baby carriages, and backpacks into service as the citizenry took to the highways. Most of these carriers were extremely heavily loaded with family valuables and keepsakes. It created a scene of pandemonium impossible to imagine.

Soldiers went door to door instructing citizens to leave. Often, they had to threaten immediate death before the occupants were convinced to abandon their homes. As SamSan sat in the Khmer Rouge truck waiting for his passengers to climb aboard, he shuddered as he witnessed a toothless old woman standing on her balcony and laughing at the Khmer Rouge soldier who yelled to her from the street, "You must leave right away, Granny. The Americans will bomb this place any minute now."

"Do not call me Granny, and I am not afraid of any old American bombs," laughed the old woman. "I have lived through bombings before, and I do not intend to leave my home and run because of a threat of bombs now."

"But Granny, you might be killed," the soldier said.

"I told you, do not call me Granny," the old woman scolded. "I have paid every one of my vows to Buddha, and he will see to it that I am looked after. This is my home, and I intend to stay right here."

SamSan watched helplessly as the soldier laughed and answered her with both words and action. "We will see if Buddha will look after you now," he said as he pulled the pin on a hand grenade and tossed it onto the balcony at the old woman's feet. The explosion that followed killed the old woman instantly, and the soldier walked away still laughing, leaving her lifeless body lying in a huge pool of blood.

As citizens left their homes by the hundreds of thousands and took to the impossibly crowded streets and highways, they often bumped into one another. Many parents lost their children in the confusion. If anyone tried to turn back or turn aside—even to look for their lost children—the soldiers first threatened bodily harm. If that person persisted in going in any direction other than the one dictated by the confused and bewildered Khmer Rouge army, the soldiers killed them in their tracks. SamSan could not hold back his tears as he watched the panicked citizens in totally disorganized exit. In his wildest imagination, he could never have dreamed of such massive chaos.

Other groups of Khmer Rouge officials began to drive their vehicles through the town with their loudspeakers repeatedly announcing, "If you were an officer in the Cambodian army, now is the time to identify yourself. We need men with leadership qualities like yours to serve in our army. We will accept you without any question and give you a commission at a one grade higher level than your present rank. If you are a first lieutenant in the Cambodian army, you will become a captain in the Khmer Rouge army; a captain will become a major, and so forth. All you need to do is come forward. We will not harm you. On the contrary—you will be welcomed into our army." They failed to mention that theirs was an army without any official rank where both soldier and leader carried the title of "Med." Even Pol Pot, the supreme leader went by the title of "Med."

SamSan felt no temptation to reveal his rank and identity. He had heard of so many treacherous tricks by the Khmer Rouge, and he knew they took pride in having an army without rank. *It is a trap*, he thought as he held his tongue.

He watched several men respond to this announcement and turn themselves in. The Khmer Rouge loaded those men into a truck, and no one ever saw them again. (Unfortunately, SamSan would learn later that his brother, Chong Ky, who had been a captain in the Cambodian army, apparently fell for this ploy and was executed.)

When his new Khmer Rouge boss returned and gave him the order to start the motor, SamSan turned the ignition key. The engine of the American-built, Cambodian Army truck, newly confiscated by the Khmer Rouge, sprung to life. As soon as they heard the sound of a motor running, several Khmer Rouge soldiers hoisted up their rifles and climbed onto the truck bed. His leader instructed SamSan to drive into the business district, and as they reached a certain location, he heard the soldiers yelling, "Stop. Stop right here!"

God Provides for His Own

He brought the truck to an abrupt standstill, and his passengers immediately jumped to the ground. One of the soldiers approached a jewelry store and placed a live hand grenade against its front door before he ran for cover. His crude door key worked to perfection, and the soldiers poured into the building to begin looting the store. SamSan stood by and observed in disbelieving silence. Most of the soldiers grabbed what SamSan considered only gaudy baubles.

"Go ahead, driver. Get some of these things for yourself," the med who acted as leader of the group said to him. "The owners of this place will not ever be coming back here. All of this merchandise belongs to the winners now."

SamSan had to brush his conscience aside as he applied his watchmaker's knowledge gained years earlier in picking six of the better quality watches from the shelves—Swiss-made brands like Titony, Omega, and Universal. He also picked a handful of quality, solid-gold rings, thinking he could use them for barter when the time came for him to leave Phnom Penh. Until this time, his prison clothes and the comb they had allowed him to keep when they booked him in jail had been his only possessions.

After he heard the admonition of the Khmer Rouge leader, SamSan felt sadly certain that the rightful owners of all Phnom Penh properties would not be returning to their homes or businesses. He felt certain that he, also, would soon be forced to join in the mass exodus from the city, and he had a pressing need to gather a few provisions for the unknown situation he faced. His conscience did not hurt quite so badly when he took a couple of changes of durable work clothes and a raincoat from the clothing store, a large bag of rice from the grocery store, and a few blankets and a large enameled boiler from the dry goods store.

The Khmer Rouge med who had charge of the group told SamSan to take a certain bed in one of the vacant houses. As soon as he established possession of his bed and room, SamSan continued his quest for supplies and took to the street where he had seen a number of abandoned chickens and pigs running free. After a spirited chase, he managed to catch a moderate-sized pig that he killed and carried back to the house. He impaled the dressed pig on a makeshift spit and roasted it over an open charcoal fire, turning it often as it cooked. While he was cooking the pig, he could not help but smile as he watched a young Khmer Rouge soldier, who sat in front of the departed family's television set and attempted to turn it on.

"Why will the damned thing not work?" the soldier swore in anger as he stared at the blank television screen.

"No electric, no TV," SamSan said with a smile.

"Damned American capitalistic junk!" screamed the soldier as he seized his heavy club and smashed the television to smithereens. "That is what I think of American capitalism."

SamSan simply smiled. He knew the TV had come from Japan.

He was able to appropriate a bicycle on the third day. After this, he mentally checked his list of things needed for his journey: *Now I have transportation to go with my clothing*, he thought. *I have rice and pork for food and a raincoat and blankets for shelter. Those are the basic things I must have to sustain life, but God has also given me some things I can use to barter on the way.*

Then he bowed his head and silently prayed, "God, You have answered my prayers and provided all my needs for my journey. But, God, You surely have taken a strange path in the way You answered those prayers. Thank You, Amen."

When he reported for work on the fourth morning, his Khmer Rouge leader said to him, "Med, you have done your job, but we do not need you anymore. Enough of our soldiers have learned to drive, so we can handle things with drivers of our own now. It is time for you to go and join all the other people from the city. You must now go to work in the fields for the good of Angkar. You must become one of the 'Old People.'"

A Search for Guek

The self-proclaimed "simple seller of noodles" was now ready and eager to start his search for Guek. He loaded all of his newly acquired supplies onto his bicycle and joined the huge throng still exiting the city. As soon as he was able, he moved away from the center of the crowd and stayed on the left side of the highway. His plan called for him to take Highway 5, which turned off to the left a short distance out of town. That highway went directly to Battambang, and he must follow it to search for Guek.

When he got to the six-kilometer marker, he found a huge crowd gathered there, still holding on to their rapidly fading hopes of returning to their homes in Phnom Penh. SamSan saw no particular reason to hurry on his forced journey, so he joined this crowd and stayed overnight.

The next morning, however, Khmer Rouge soldiers gave the crowd specific and pointed instructions that they must continue on their journey away from Phnom Penh. They made the point obvious and final—there would be no return to the city. They further indicated there would be no more tolerance of slower than necessary travel, and certainly, no tolerance at all of refusal to travel.

"All of you are what we call 'New People.'" Their preaching reverberated repeatedly in almost intolerable decibels. "You are city dwellers and worthless to our new society. You cannot even raise your own bread. In the new society, everyone will produce crops from the ground. You must become "Old People,' and learn to work with your hands to produce crops, or you must die in the process.

"Every one of you 'New People' must remember that this is now a fact of life in Cambodia: 'To keep you is of no benefit to us. To destroy you is no loss.'" This slogan would be repeated to the trudging masses hundreds of times each week for many weeks to come.

Even in the crushing crowd, the young Cambodian felt terribly alone. *I must find Guek so I can look after her during this terrible time*, he thought.

Time and again he tried to turn onto Highway 5 toward her family home. On each attempt to turn aside toward Battambang, a Khmer Rouge soldier made threatening gestures with his rifle as he confronted the anxious wife-seeker and demanded, "Where do you think you are going?"

"To Battambang to look for wife," he replied.

His plea fell on deaf ears on each occasion, and he heard the same words again and again, "You stay in line with others, or we bury you right here." He finally yielded to these threats and abandoned his effort to look for Guek. He reluctantly followed the mass of humanity on Highway 6 toward Siem Riep.

A Family Is Formed

The Khmer Rouge soldiers began to pressure the teeming crowd to speed up their exit from the city. Any effort to stop and rest brought a sharp lash with a strap or a prod from a Khmer Rouge rifle. As he dealt with the pain from his aching muscles, SamSan tried to find something he could be thankful for besides simply being alive, out of prison, and having some provisions. Try as hard as he might, he could only come up with, *Thank God this is not the rainy season.*

The Khmer Rouge pushed the massive crowd to continue the journey until dark had completely settled in. As he set up his camp in the black of night, SamSan felt what he thought was a tree stump. Totally exhausted, he sat down on the ground and leaned his back against the stump for support and went to sleep. All through the night, he was keenly aware of a foul odor in the area, but he thought it came from the fetid fish that Muslims in that area dried for food. He also felt what he thought were ants crawling on his body. However, the light of day revealed his "stump" to be a human corpse that had become completely rigid from rigor mortis, and the "ants" were actually maggots from that corpse.

SamSan's first reaction to this discovery was predictable. He vomited; then he hurried to immerse himself in the Mekong River to bathe and wash his clothes, while a fellow traveler watched his bicycle and other possessions. Even after his thorough bathing and change of clothes, it took several days before he felt completely free of the terrible odor.

By this stage in the perilous journey, the travelers had abandoned all trucks and automobiles because of mechanical problems, lack of fuel, or unnavigable terrain. Khmer Rouge soldiers had commandeered a few of them. SamSan could travel more rapidly than most refugees because he rode a bicycle and had very few possessions. He passed party after pitiful party as they stumbled forward with oxcarts, handcarts, and bicycles or backpacks all loaded with their meager possessions. The group had covered about twenty kilometers when they came near the small village of So Kuon. Here SamSan saw what he considered the most pitiful family of all the ones he had seen, and it touched his heart.

The father, an old man SamSan estimated to be well over sixty, appeared to be gravely ill. He staggered and fell frequently in spite of his wife's constant efforts to support him. Every jolting step he took appeared to be causing excruciating pain in his lower belly. In an obvious effort to lessen the pain, the old man held onto his lower abdomen with both of his hands. Hearing him cry out from the severe pain in his abdomen and seeing him stumble every few steps in spite of his wife's best efforts to steady him brought great emotional pain to the sympathetic young Cambodian.

Because it took both of her parents to keep her father moving forward, their daughter, only a little younger than SamSan, had to push the overloaded bicycle onto which the family had lashed most of their possessions. She appeared to be having a difficult time in doing this. SamSan pulled his bicycle alongside the afflicted family and offered to help them.

"Hello," he said to the father, "I am Ly Peing (using his childhood nickname as he had planned, but dropping the feigned ignorance). I can see you are having a lot of pain when you walk. I would like to help you if you will allow me. Would you like to share some of my rice and pork with me?"

"I am glad to meet you, Peing," said the old man. "I am Lor Sieng, and this is my wife, Tang Siam, and our daughter, Lor Huy Keng. It is very kind of you to offer to help us, and we will be happy to accept your offer of assistance and food. Apparently, you can see that we cannot continue this journey for long the way things are going for me right now, and it very thoughtful of you to offer us some help."

After the group had eaten, SamSan placed Lor Sieng on the luggage rack of his bicycle and carried him for a distance of about two kilometers. He propped the old man up in the shade of a mango tree and made him as comfortable as possible. The Good Samaritan was about to return to give Tang Siam and Huy Keng some help in catching up, when a Khmer Rouge soldier, who had been staring at him for a good while, suddenly confronted him with a menacing sneer.

"I know you, you capitalistic demon," snarled the soldier as he came face-to-face with SamSan. "You tour guide for SOKHAR Voyages in Phnom Penh, and you help American military. You enemy of our people. You not deserve to live." The soldier raised his rifle to his shoulder and aimed it directly at SamSan's head.

SamSan had rehearsed a response for a situation such as this, but he was petrified with fright by the suddenness of the incident. His tongue seemed frozen. His practiced response would not come out immediately, and he resigned himself to the fact that his time had come.

Before he could gain his composure and speak, Lor Sieng calmly answered the irate soldier. "You are mistaken, my friend. Everyone knows that the royal family owns SOKHAR Voyages and that all of their tour guides are government employees. There is an ironclad rule in this country that no person of Chinese origin can work for any branch of the Cambodian government. This man is my son, and I am Chinese, so it would not have been possible for him to be a SOKHAR guide. Most oriental people do have a lot of common characteristics, and we do sometimes look a great deal like one another. You have made a natural mistake. Do not worry about it."

By this time, SamSan could speak for himself. Using the broken Khmer with a feigned heavy Chinese accent he had so diligently practiced in recent days, he said, "Me not tour guide. Me sell noodles."

When the gullible soldier lowered his rifle and left, SamSan breathed a long sigh of relief. Then, he turned to Lor Sieng and said, "Thank God, and thank you, my friend. That was what I call quick thinking and a great answer in a tough situation. I was so frightened I absolutely could not speak. Perhaps God had it planned that way; because your answer fit the situation so perfectly."

Then he added, "By the way, this makes the third time in my life that being 'adopted' has saved my skin in one way or another." He told Lor Sien about his birth and his false birth certificate.

Still visibly upset from the frightening confrontation, SamSan returned to help Tang Siam and Huy Keng carry their heavy loads to the spot where Lor Sieng waited. They repeated this "leap-frog" procedure three times that day before the quartet stopped to rest for the night.

After a second day of SamSan's leapfrog transporting of Lor Sieng, then returning for his wife and daughter, the old man seemed to be in terrible pain when his new young friend tried to bed him down. As SamSan made him as comfortable as possible, the seriously ill man asked him to come closer. "I can see from your actions that you are a good man," he said. "I know that I am about to die, and my death cannot be far away under these circumstances. There is no expert medical help available any longer because the Khmer Rouge have closed all of our hospitals and killed most of our doctors and nurses. Folks tell me they have only kept a few untrained so-called nurses who practice old-time country, herbal, medicine.

"And I do not expect my wife to last long after I am gone, because she is also in poor health. I know it is asking a lot from you, but I want you to promise me right now that you will look after our daughter when both of us are dead."

"Me?" SamSan's tone of voice showed great surprise. "You hardly know me." Nevertheless, he knew this was the request of a dying man, and he found it difficult to refuse him.

"Yes, you," Lor Sieng replied. "I have seen enough to know you are a good man. Please say you will do it. You are my only hope."

"But I am a married man," SamSan objected. "How can I make a promise to look after your daughter? That would not be right."

"I am not asking you to marry her," said Lor Sieng. "I am asking you to promise to look after her when we are gone. She is still young and has never been through any real difficulties. She will surely die, or the Khmer Rouge will kill her if someone does not look after her. She has some very valuable things with her and can compensate you very well. Will you make that promise to me?"

"Sir, I-I will do the best I can, but I am not looking for any pay," the young Cambodian stammered as he turned to leave. When he returned with Tang Siam and Huy Keng, the quartet made camp for the night.

SamSan and his new friends had spent two and a half miserable weeks on their forced journey when they caught up with a larger group who were resting on the edge of a rice paddy, apparently with Khmer Rouge permission. By this time, the old man's pain had become absolutely unbearable. He could not walk, his breath had become quite short, and his abdomen felt almost as hard as a rock. When Keng made the visit to the rice supply truck for the group's daily food ration, she happened to make contact with a Khmer Rouge nurse.

"My father is very sick, and it looks like he is about to die," she said to the nurse. "Will you please come and do something for him?"

The nurse rode a bicycle to visit Lor Sieng. After she had examined the patient briefly, she gave him a shot of some unknown medicine and a small bottle of green medicine to take by mouth. She did not give the family any information about what diagnosis she made or what drugs she had used.

"He be okay when medicines work," the nurse promised the family as she mounted her bicycle to leave.

Within ten minutes after the nurse gave Lor Sieng the shot, the old man screamed with pain and gasped his last breath. His skin turned such a dark blue color, there could be no question he was dead. Keng's tears flowed in a massive stream, and her mournful wail echoed throughout the area.

"She killed him!" the grieving daughter screamed hysterically. "That old nurse killed my daddy! She gave him a shot of something to put him out of his misery instead of something to make him well, and then she told us he would be okay. Why did I ever call her in the first place? Daddy said those Khmer Rouge nurses were not any good."

SamSan's persistent and well-reasoned protests could not quiet Keng's loud grieving. "At least he is not suffering such terrible pain anymore," he said. "Your father knew he was dying, and he told me so the first day I met him. He made me promise that I would look after you and your mother when he was gone, and that is exactly what I intend to do. Please, Keng, do not cry, and try not to worry. We have our own lives and your mother's life to protect. These are dangerous times."

He might as well have spoken to the wind.

SamSan asked the Khmer Rouge cadre for permission to leave the group long enough to bury Lor Sieng in the woods close to a nearby rice paddy. He pawned one of his gold rings as security to borrow a hoe from a local "old citizen." After he had dug the grave, he lashed Lor Sieng's body to the frame of his bicycle and managed to give the old man one last ride to the gravesite for burial. He marked the grave with a makeshift cross that he fashioned out of pieces of wood tied together with vines and drove into the ground at the head of the grave. He hoped the marker would help the family find the gravesite again if they should ever return to that place.

A Chance for Escape?

The Khmer Rouge permitted the family to stay there for about five days, sleeping in a bombed-out house. One day when SamSan made the trip to the rice supply truck to get his group's meager food allot-ment, he was pleasantly surprised to see his old commanding offi-cer, General Ith Suong, sitting under an umbrella in the center of town. He had disguised himself as a Buddhist monk by dressing in an orange robe with a hood pulled over his freshly shaved head. SamSan's reflex action was to snap to attention and give his former commander a salute.

"I am glad to see you, Boss," he said, using the familiar title for the general he had only used in private conversation with the general before that time.

Ith Suong reacted swiftly to SamSan's signs of recognition. He shook his head slightly from side-to-side and put a finger to his lips to call for quiet. "Do not call me 'Boss,'" he whispered. "Call me 'Brother,' and for goodness sake do not salute me. Do you want to get both of us killed?"

The pair then put their heads together for quiet conversation. "Soma, I am surprised you would even speak to me, let alone salute me, since I did not make any contact when you were in prison," the general said. " Ek Preong threatened my life if I interfered in any way in your case. I hope you will forgive me."

"I forgave you as soon as I got out of prison, Brother. Right after the Khmer Rouge released me, it dawned on me that my being in the prison when they took over was what saved my life. They assumed I was a Khmer Rouge sympathizer, so they let me go without asking any questions," SamSan replied.

"I know that you worship Buddha, but I am a Christian. I believe my God intended for all of the efforts to fail where my friends tried to get me out of prison. If the Khmer Rouge had found me in my home or in my office, they would have killed me right then. I believe God kept me in that prison so I could walk out of there alive and unharmed."

"That is an interesting theory, and I suppose it could be true," Ith Suong whispered to SamSan. "By the way, a group of my friends is planning to attempt an escape very soon. Would you be interested in joining us?"

"That is pretty risky under these circumstances, is it not, General?" SamSan asked.

"I do not believe it is as risky as staying here in this rat race run by mad men," said the general. "In fact, now may be the absolutely best time to try it—before they get well organized. How long do you think it will be before someone else recognizes me the way you did—someone who is not my friend? You know I am a marked man, and I suspect you are about as high on their wanted list as I am, my friend."

"I know what you mean about being recognized, sir," SamSan responded. "Just a few days ago, one of the Khmer Rouge soldiers recognized me from my days at SOKHAR Voyages. If my new Chinese friend had not thought quickly and claimed me as his son and reminded that soldier that no Chinese could work for a government agency, I am sure I would not be alive today. As it was, it scared me half to death."

"You did not answer my question, Soma," said the general. "Do you or do you not want to join us in our escape? I feel I owe you the chance to come with us because I did not help you in prison. I need to know quickly, because the escape is coming down very soon. We have a map, a compass, and a trustworthy guide who knows the jungle. We also have some money and quite a few supplies. I still have some connections in France, and our plan is to go there. Do you or do you not want to come with us?"

"You bet I would like to go, Brother," SamSan answered, "but I made a promise to a dying man the other day. I told him I would look after his daughter, and I must honor that promise. Let me speak with her and her mother to see if they would like to go with you. As for myself, I am ready."

Ith Suong made no reply as SamSan turned to leave. He immediately consulted with Keng and her mother, who agreed to join the general. However, by the time the young Cambodian returned to inform the general they would like to join his party, the general had disappeared. Although SamSan felt disappointed, he understood that a person whose name stood near the top of a Khmer Rouge hit list could not trust anyone in a dangerous time like this—not even a former faithful aide-de-camp. He was happy to hear later that the general had succeeded in escaping to France.

A Commune Is Formed

The soldiers soon forced SamSan, Keng, and Tang Siam to return to the highway, rejoin the retreating masses, and continue their seemingly endless journey toward an unknown destination. Nearly fifty kilometers after they passed the small town of So Kuon, the Khmer Rouge soldiers began to separate the travelers randomly into groups of several hundred people. They directed one of these soon-to-be communes down each small pig trail that intersected Highway 6 and into the surrounding jungle. Each group received an assignment to a different area of the jungle, but there seemed to be no real pattern to their deployment.

The new, haphazardly colonized commune that included SamSan, Keng, and her mother went down a narrow country road that led into the jungle near the tiny village of Kom Pong K Dey. The only instructions they received when the soldiers first herded them like cattle into a small, densely forested area were, "This will be the home of your commune."

"I do not like the situation we are in," SamSan said to his companions, "but, after two horrible months of wandering like Moses in the wilderness, at least we are not being aimlessly driven farther away from Phnom Penh. The best thing that happened to us so far is that we got here just before the monsoon season starts. Just think about how tough it would have been if we had to travel in the monsoons."

In this new jungle setting, each family group set up camp with whatever equipment they had. Those with no provisions had to sleep on the ground. Some had brought thin mats, which they used as beds, while some had the luxury of having brought hammocks. SamSan's new charges strung up some of their blankets for privacy and used others as bedding. Mosquitoes were everywhere, and the trio had no protection from their irritating and dangerous, incessant bites.

The Khmer Rouge provided no sanitary facilities for the people, and there were no tools to dig them in the jungle. Hundreds of people used the surrounding jungle without any waste disposal plan. After a week, the odor became almost unbearable and innumerable flies added to their intense discomfort. The beginning of the rainy season with its sweltering moist heat further compounded their problems. SamSan built a small, flimsy brush hut with a thatched roof to gain some protection from the inhumane elements. It was the best he could do under those trying circumstances without any tools.

After a few days, a detail from the Khmer Rouge came to the area bringing instructions about the general policies of the Khmer Rouge for the entire assembled group: "Let me remind you that you are what we call 'new citizens,' and are of no real value to Angkar," the speaker said. "You must become 'old citizens' or die in the attempt. You must always cooperate with Angkar and never criticize your leadership. Any criticism is punishable by death. You must report any subversive activity or even questionable acts or statements by any person, regardless of who he or she might be. Children, let me remind you that it is your duty to report any word or action by your parents or grandparents that might be harmful to Angkar.

"Everyone must work regardless of your age or the state of your health. We will immediately eliminate from the commune any person who does not work, and there will be no trial. We cannot afford to feed nonproductive parasites. The only exceptions made to this rule will be for the smallest children. Angkar will take them for early instruction in the ways of our society. We need children. They can and must receive training to be the reliable basis for our society in years to come.

"You no longer have any personal possessions. Everything that exists around you belongs to Angkar. You have no family and you have no God except Angkar. You owe all of your allegiance to Angkar. Angkar will select your mates and rear your children for you. We will not tolerate any signs of affection for any person or the worship of any god. We will not tolerate any sign of sorrow or grief, no love songs or religious songs, and none of the decadent western literature or the lies of religion. These are signs of allegiance to something or someone other than Angkar and are punishable by immediate death. As I said, your sole allegiance and love is due to Angkar. Do you understand?"

A subdued murmur went through the crowd, but no one dared to speak aloud.

The speaker continued, "Now, about your work assignments: First of all, the land where you are staying must be cleared to make a rice paddy field to help feed the people of Angkar. You must accomplish this goal quickly or you are likely to become quite hungry. We expect every man to cut down a minimum of two or three trees every day until you have cleared the area. Your overseers will see that you do it, or else.

"The women will receive work assignments on the local rice-paddy dam. You will work seven days a week. Those days of rest are a thing of the decadent past. You will receive more detailed work instructions from your village head [an appointed civilian director of the village corresponding to a mayor] and his assistants very soon."

SamSan received an axe as his only tool for his task of cutting two or three huge trees each day. When he asked for a whetstone to sharpen his axe, his Khmer Rouge overseer said to him, "Find your own rock."

One day, a sudden gust of wind caused a tree he had cut to fall in an unexpected direction. A limb from the tree struck the inexperienced woodsman and knocked him down, pinning him to the ground. By summoning every ounce of his strength, he finally worked himself free, but he sustained a painful shoulder injury. "One foot closer, and

I would have died," he explained to Keng when he finally dragged himself home. His overseer still expected him to continue working and cut his minimum of two trees every day in spite of his injury.

It angered SamSan that the Khmer Rouge supplied each person with only one cup of rice each day, in spite of the fact that they demanded heavy work from that laborer. Angkar provided no vegetables and no meat, yet killing an animal for food was a capital crime, because Angkar considered any animal to be of more value than a human being. There was also danger in picking any fruits from the trees, because all fruits and vegetables were "the property of Angkar."

The Khmer Rouge regarded the picking of any of them for personal use as stealing. Anyone caught in the act would be punished by death. Adding to the danger, many of the fruits and leaves of the plants were poisonous, and the city dwellers did not recognize them. Therefore, many people suffered from food poisoning and quite a few died, especially from eating poison mushrooms. Hunger drove SamSan to risk his life many times by disregarding the Khmer Rouge restrictions.

Using the jungle survival lessons he learned in his durian importing days, he climbed trees and gathered food, especially mangos. The many bites he received from huge ants that lived in the trees actually served as more of a deterrent to his fruit and nut gathering than did his fear of the Khmer Rouge. He sometimes even resorted to begging rice from the "old people" who lived nearby and was thrilled when these farmers occasionally allowed him to pick a few peppers from their fields.

The group became terribly frustrated trying to catch enough water from the rain in their few containers, especially when mosquito larvae showed up in their precious water supply so quickly. Yet, they knew of no source of fresh water until someone discovered an old well in the area. SamSan did note that the water had a greenish color, but they joyfully took water from this well to use for both drinking and cooking. After the commune had used the water for a week or so, someone discovered a few human hairs in their water container, and they realized the Khmer Rouge had disposed of one or more bodies in that well. That finding spelled the end to their so-called "fresh" water. Hundreds of people had drunk that water, and its contamination could possibly have caused some of their sicknesses and even some deaths.

A few weeks after the group's arrival in the jungle, Keng's mother became seriously ill. Her fever-wracked body shook with chills, and she complained of being extremely cold despite the oppressive heat. SamSan and Keng assumed she had malaria, but they had no medicines to give her for its treatment. SamSan knew about cinchona bark as a treatment, but those trees grew only in South America. He did not know of any remedy that existed in this jungle.

Because she did not receive adequate food and absolutely no medical treatment, Tang Siam weakened rapidly and died after the group had been in the jungle for about a month. For the second time within less than four months, SamSan buried one of Keng's parents in a grave that he had dug. The next day, the Khmer Rouge carried Keng away to her assignment, working on a dam to retain water for the rice paddy.

An Illicit Love?

As soon as Keng left the camp, a great sense of loneliness overwhelmed SamSan, and it caught him completely by surprise. Love had not been in the equation when he promised Lor Sieng he would look after their daughter when the old couple died. A married man with a living wife should never harbor thoughts about another woman such as he had about Keng. He felt guilty... dirty. An emotion like love was not supposed to happen in a situation like this—but the feeling persisted.

His motives had been absolutely pure when he stopped to help Keng and her family during their panicked flight from Phnom

Penh, even though he could not help but notice how attractive she appeared at the time. Nothing physical had ever happened between them except for a few wistful glances on his part. *Why should the feeling of loneliness be so intense at this time? What did it mean?*

He wondered, *was it possible he would never see Guek again? It certainly appeared that way now with absolutely no way of travel or communication available except to the military and the most elite of the Khmer Rouge. He had tried diligently to go to her, but the Khmer Rouge had forced him to go to Siem Riep. Their separation was certainly not his fault.*

Guek was so delicate. Could she even have survived if the Khmer Rouge put her through the same ordeal as they did the people from Phnom Penh? The questions seemed endless.

Had true love reared its beautiful head in this ugly situation? Was this God's plan? Did Keng feel the same way as he felt? This feeling toward another woman had not been included in his plans, nor did it fit in well with the code that Angkar had laid out for all citizens. "Angkar must be your only love," they had said.

When Keng came back to the commune after about three weeks, SamSan could hardly believe how much weight she had lost in such a short time or how pale she appeared even though she had been working outside. Regardless of the fact that he could read the evidence to the contrary, he said with a broad smile, "I hope things went well with you while you were away."

"Oh, SamSan," she said through her tears, "it has been awful. You were not there to tell me what to do, and the Khmer Rouge do not know how to do anything. They have killed all the engineers and professionals who know the proper way to build dams and other things. One bulldozer and two or three trucks could have done in one or two days what a thousand of us women did in three weeks.

"But the Khmer Rouge have parked every machine and siphoned the gas out of them to start fires or run the motorcycles of the big bosses. They called it 'decadent capitalism' to use any of the bulldozers and trucks they captured from the Cambodian army or to use any modern equipment in their work. Most of the time in my job, I carried two baskets of dirt suspended from a don rek. Sometimes I walked as much as two kilometers to empty the small amount of dirt I could carry in my baskets onto the dam. There were times when we even passed handfuls of dirt from hand to hand over long distances. They did not care what happened to us."

SamSan could no longer restrain himself. He overcame his inhibitions, held her firmly in his arms, and kissed her. "But I care a lot about what happens to you, and to us, my darling," he said.

Keng eagerly returned his embrace and giggled delightedly for the first time since SamSan had met her. The love scene that followed relieved many of the tensions the preceding months of terror had built up, and the two lovers became truly one.

In the discussion that followed this impetuous action, SamSan reasoned, "It appears to me that, with the way we have been brought together and left alone—and especially since we have had no choice in the matter—God intends for us to be together. I cannot foresee any possible way for me to rejoin Guek, because the Khmer Rouge do not allow anyone to travel, and they do not care if families are split up. Furthermore, they seem to assume we are already man and wife. We have both noticed that families seem to get better treatment than unmarried individuals. Why should we not carry on as husband and wife?"

Keng raised no objection, and they agreed to continue their intimate roles.

A few days after Keng's return to the commune, Chang Ngy You, an elderly Chinese "old citizen," contacted the local Khmer Rouge officials and petitioned for permission to bring several Chinese "new citizens" into their village to live with his family. He had formerly served as school principal and teacher in the school in Kom Pong K Dey, and he staunchly defended racial separation. He had formed a Chinese Citizens Committee many years earlier, and still served as its chairman with his older son, Chang Uy Kuong, as vice-chairman.

Surprisingly, the local Khmer Rouge officials showed enough respect for Mr. Chang to grant his request.

The following day, a cart pulled by two oxen came to transport SamSan and Keng, along with two other couples with their four children, into the village. The three families moved into the old school building, where SamSan and Keng thought it seemed like heaven to sleep on a table and have some privacy. They still went to work daily at their assigned jobs. SamSan quickly became fast friends with Chang Kok Kuong, the second son of the elder Mr. Chang.

SamSan then swapped one of his watches to an "old citizen" for a water buffalo, and he had the animal butchered. He traded some of the meat for rice. Then he gave a huge party for the Chinese Citizens' Association to show his appreciation for the help they had given to his family. The thought even went through his mind, *Perhaps our situation here may not be so bad after all.*

However, the relatively good situation existed only because the Khmer Rouge in Kom Pong K Dey had not attained good organization this early in their time of absolute power, and the local communes were not yet strictly enforcing some of the changes Angkar had decreed for the entire country. The Khmer Rouge had intentionally destroyed all radio, telephone, and other communication services, so word reached Kom Pong K Dey at a snail's pace. The system in force in his commune at the particular moment allowed SamSan to leave his work after he had felled three trees.

The Khmer Rouge had abandoned all forms of money, so barter remained as the only available system for any type of trade. He viewed this situation as an opportunity for profit, so he swapped the second of his watches for a horse and still another watch, his third, for five kilos of tobacco.

Any time he could steal off from work, he used to ride his horse from village to village trading tobacco for rice, meat, and watermelon from the "old citizens" who had not yet felt the horribly hard heel of the Khmer Rouge system. To bypass the Khmer Rouge rules that prohibited travel between villages, he obtained a "permission to travel note" from the Chinese Citizens' Association of Kom Pong K Dey. These early barter sessions proved to be very profitable.

The Policy Toughens

The Khmer Rouge policy quickly toughened, and they abolished the Chinese Citizens' Association as well as all forms of trading and possession of personal property. All people were required to work long hours each day in establishing the communal rice paddy fields. All of the results of their labor belonged to Angkar in return for the empty promise that they would supply whatever need each citizen had.

Even the local "old citizens" were now included under the same harsh rules as the "new citizens." All "old citizens" of foreign extraction became slave laborers and worked under the same conditions and restrictions as "new citizens." They also now lived under the same constant reminder of the motto of the Khmer Rouge: *To keep you is of no benefit to us. To destroy you is no loss.*

After enduring seemingly endless hours of oppressive daytime work, every person in the commune was compelled to stay awake through long commune meetings in oppressively hot tents at night. Boring speaker after boring speaker droned on and on in excessively amplified monotone through the loudspeakers. They admonished all citizens to perform for the glory of Angkar: "You may rely on Angkar to care for your every need. We have founded this society on the abilities of human beings and not on machines. Everyone will be required to produce and we will not tolerate idleness, nor will we use any tractors or trucks or other instruments of decadent capitalism.

"You must do exactly as you are commanded at all times and without question or you will face the possibility of death. If you work hard and show a love for Angkar, you should not have a problem. However, we will not tolerate any criticism of Angkar by anyone at any time. In fact, we will eliminate from the system anyone who criticizes the system. You must never forget that you are 'new citizens' and are useless to us unless you truly become 'old citizens.' Never forget the rule by which you must live: *To keep you is of no benefit to us. To destroy you is no loss.* May Angkar live long and prosper."

Someone reported to the authorities that an "old citizen" named Kow Cheak, a vice president of the Chinese Citizens' Association, had said, "It is crazy for us to have to travel by oxcart in this modern, rapid age." He soon vanished from the scene, and everyone presumed he was dead.

"So much for any hope of more help from the Chinese Citizens' Association," SamSan remarked to Keng, "It is back to the old and dangerous square one again. We cannot trust anyone."

SLAVE LABOR
Siem Riep Province, Cambodia—Late 1975 to Late 1978

"Chalad!"

The word brought great fear to the normally fearless SamSan. *Chalad* was the Cambodian term for the horrible migrant work details that required the slave laborers to be away from their families for two or three months at a time and to work in inhuman conditions.

The Khmer Rouge required these captives to live in primitive camps near their worksite. They had no sanitary facilities or protection from mosquitoes and no malaria prevention material, techniques, or medicines. Every person in the camp had to work at least twelve hours a day without a break. To make it more difficult for the laborers to formulate any escape plans, they assigned each individual to a different work group almost every day.

Even with such hard labor for such long hours, a worker received only one or two cupfuls of thin rice gruel per day. Not surprisingly, several members of each of these *chalad* groups failed to return to their families at the end of their sessions. The Khmer Rouge killed some who were trying to escape and some for disobeying orders, while many more died from disease or starvation or from the inhuman conditions of their work.

SamSan would do almost anything to avoid *chalad*.

When the first opportunity arose, he went to the village director and carried one of the fine Swiss watches he had managed to hide until this time. "Me have for you one present," he said to the official as he presented the timepiece. "Is one Universal watch. Is very fine watch from Switzerland. Me not high person, me not wear. You high person, you wear. If watch break, me fix. In fact, me fix almost anything what broke."

He hoped his gift would bring him to the village director's attention and the awareness of his skills at repairing watches and other things would result in his assignment to work that would keep him near the village. That way he could work on watches for the soldiers and commune officials. After all, almost every Khmer Rouge soldier had at least one watch he or she had "liberated" from a victim's corpse somewhere. Most of these watches were cheap, and they were getting old. It stood to reason that many of them had to be in need of some type of repair.

The village director immediately appointed SamSan as the unofficial watchmaker and fix-it man for the village. He had no spare parts and no fine watchmaker tools, but he could clean their watches with a duck's feather and oil them with rifle oil. That simple action would repair a majority of those minute machines if the mainspring remained intact.

By this time, the commune had constructed open-pit toilets that stood in need of cleaning out from time to time. The Village Director also assigned SamSan and his friend, Kok Kuong, to clean out these toilets and spread the feces out over a drying area. When the material they had spread out became dry, they dug it up, along with a small amount of dirt and carried it to the fields to serve as fertilizer.

Many people might consider it no great favor to be given such a task, but after two or three months on this job, the watchmaker failed to even notice the fecal odor, and he still did not have to suffer the hardships and dangers of *chalad*. SamSan considered those benefits and decided he had made a wonderful trade.

As an added benefit to his job, although he broke stringent rules and risked his life to do it, he managed to maintain a small, secret vegetable garden on the edge of the field of drying feces. From that source, he could sometimes clandestinely share a portion of its produce with his elderly neighbors.

SamSan apparently became a true favorite of the village director at the commune in Kom Pong K Dey, and the young seller of noodles could not completely understand the reason for it. *Surely he does not show me this much favoritism just because of the watch I gave him*, SamSan mused. *I wonder about him. He seems to know more about me than he is letting on. It is creepy—as if he is thinking I might be of some value to him by putting him in touch with some of my contacts if he decides to defect some day.*

I keep hearing there is a lot of infighting going on with the higher brass in the Communist Party, and they have done some house cleaning. It does not really matter what his reason is. I will take all the favoritism I can get, but I will keep my eyes open and try to stay out of trouble.

The director had even overheard a conversation where SamSan spoke French with a resident in the commune. This evidence of some degree of education could have easily been a death warrant, but the director had only asked him, "Where did you learn to speak French?"

"Oh, neighbor, he speak French. Me learn from his children," SamSan replied nonchalantly.

Chang Ngy You, the former head of the Chinese Citizens' Association, saw the evidence of the village director's preferential treatment for SamSan and spoke to him about it. "The village director seems to like you and give you special treatment. Will you ask him about ending the edict where Angkar forces Chinese people to marry people of other races? It is against every principle we have ever lived by."

When SamSan broached the question to the village director, he received a very quick and pointed answer, "Angkar gave the order for those marriages, and it cannot be countermanded. Angkar will continue to assign wives to men as it sees fit. Furthermore, we will soon move Chinese families—even the ones classified as 'old citizen' families—into various villages. They will be separated from one another so they cannot easily plan a rebellion. Only one Chinese family will be allowed in each village."

Although the village director had appeared irked by SamSan's question about interracial marriage, he promoted him from the "honey wagon" and assigned him to raise hogs for Angkar. This job allowed him and Keng to live in a bamboo house with a thatched roof the commune had built over a portion of the pigpen. From twenty to thirty pigs at a time were assigned to him, and he fed them with rice husks until they became adult animals before he turned them back over to village authorities. Regular hog-wire surrounded a majority of the pigpen, but a smaller area of the pen had only a thick hedgerow that served as a barrier for the porcine animals.

On one particularly frightening occasion, the pigs rooted under the hedgerow and all of them escaped. SamSan prayed constantly that no one would steal a free-running pig, because the officials had warned him that any one of the animals held a much higher value in the eyes of Angkar than he or any human being. He was able to round up all of his charges quickly, with one exception. He knew that if he could not find the missing porker, Angkar would accuse him of having eaten a pig and arranged the escape of the others to cover up that deed. He looked everywhere for his runaway but could not find him. He prayed fervently for God to help him out of a situation where he faced a very real possibility of death. Immediately after that prayer, he heard the distant grunting of the pig in the jungle. He breathed a prayer of thanks to God as he rounded up the last escapee and repaired the hole in the hedgerow.

A Fire and a Tribunal

The Khmer Rouge wished for their populace to live by the work of human hands, not by any machines. Cambodia had no electrical power because her leaders had destroyed every power plant in the country—they considered electricity a symbol of decadent capitalism. Therefore, SamSan made a candle from a hollowed-out section of bamboo filled with tree sap to light his way around the darkened house at night. A wick immersed into the tree sap could then be easily lighted and extinguished. One night as he went to bed, he routinely snuffed out his candle and stored it in its usual place. Unfortunately, as he slept that night, the wind apparently caused the still-smoldering candlewick to reignite in those close quarters. SamSan woke up to find his house ablaze. Despite a village-wide bucket brigade, his house was a total loss.

His trial before the village tribunal on a charge of negligence in causing the fire was a fearsome thing. His life and his position were on the line one more time. For some reason, the tribunal gave him another chance and the villagers rebuilt his house, but the village director gave his hog-raising assignment to a different family and demoted SamSan and Keng to the usual hovel provided for "new citizens."

In his new assignment, SamSan collected nectar from palm tree blossoms. The Khmer Rouge used this nectar in making sugar. In this detail, he placed his life at risk several times every day as he climbed up the tall, and somewhat fragile, palm trees with no safety equipment. He used a knife to put a small nick in the stamen of each palm blossom. Then he skillfully hung a bamboo tube in such a way that the nectar from the blossom dripped into it.

The next morning, he would return to climb each tree again, collect the tubes full of nectar and replace them with empty tubes. He would put fifteen or twenty full tubes on each end of a bamboo don rek to carry the nectar to the cooking vat, where an old woman cooked it until it reached a very thick, syrupy consistency. When the boiling liquid cooled, it formed crystals and solidified into sugar. He managed to pilfer small amounts of this sugar from time to time to supplement his and Keng's pitifully poor diet.

Although SamSan's assigned tasks had changed several times, Keng continued to work on the rice-paddy dam or in the completed rice fields. One day, she fainted on the job. Any incident that resulted in a work stoppage usually brought a sentence of death on the spot. Quite contrary to the usual way of handling such cases, her supervisor brought her back to her quarters and did not require her to work in the fields anymore. The village director changed her assignment, and she became the seamstress for the village. In her new job, she made and/or repaired uniforms for the Khmer Rouge soldiers and the civilian communist leaders.

After seeing Keng's preferential treatment, SamSan became optimistic once again for the well-being of his family, although he continued to be worried about the reason for Keng's fainting in the first place. If she were truly ill, he knew he could not find competent medical advice in Cambodia. The Khmer Rouge had wiped out every vestige of western medicine and killed anyone guilty of practicing it. For the time being, he could only watch, wait, and hope for the best. His wait did not last very long. In just a few days, a missed period confirmed the fact that Keng was pregnant. This news brought a remarkably mixed bag of emotions to the expectant couple.

"I have always wanted a child," SamSan said to Keng, "but I never dreamed of its happening in a time and situation like we are in right now. What will we do when the time comes that the Khmer Rouge send the child rearers to take our baby away? I think it would kill us to have our child taken from us and raised in the Khmer Rouge philosophy that both of us hate so much."

"That worries me too," Keng said as her tears flowed freely. "But what really worries me most is, do I have enough strength to carry this baby to term and deliver him while we are being fed as little as they are allowing us now? I do not want my baby to die, and I certainly do not want to die either."

"I want you both to live, and I will do everything in my power to help you," SamSan replied as he daubed her eyes with a rag. "But for right now, we had better dry these tears. You remember what the man said."

He began to speak in a high, mocking voice, "'Shedding tears mean you are unhappy with Angkar and that you do not wish to live here. We will be most happy to grant you that wish.'"

"The only thing we can do now is to trust in God to work things out for us, no matter how bad the situation gets. We must pray and keep a smile on our faces in spite of our problems. Under these circumstances, God is our only hope."

"You are right," said Keng as she forced a fake smile. "We cannot do anything more than that right now. So we just have to keep up the pretense of being happy if we are to stay alive."

Chalad

Keng's pregnancy had advanced to about six months when the couple received the disheartening news: Every male in the commune above nine years of age must go on *chalad*. A form of blight had produced an emergency condition for the rice crop for the entire region, and the people had to gather it promptly or it would be lost. The chalad order had come directly from Angkar, and no village director had enough power to countermand the order for any individual. SamSan could not escape this assignment.

He left for his dreaded duty in the middle months of the rainy season of what he calculated to be the year 1977. Time had meant nothing to any of these slave laborers since their captivity began. No calendars were ever on display, and they had no reason to keep up with the days and months. Every day seemed exactly like the day before, with the exception of April 17.

On that date, the Khmer Rouge had seized control of Cambodia, and it became the only celebrated date on the entire calendar. On April 17 each year, they gave a huge feast for the entire country, including chicken, pork and water buffalo. Every person in the country could eat as much as he or she wanted to eat, and each one got one new work garment on that day. SamSan could remember attending only two of these festivals since he had left Phnom Penh in April 1975, so he calculated that the present date must be fairly near the end of 1977.

After his arrival at the chalad work camp, SamSan found that, as he had expected, the working conditions were almost unbearable. They were in the rice paddies before sun-up and required to work until they could hardly see to find their way back to the camp. The monsoon rains and the short, steamy, hot periods between those showers added to their discomforts. He sweated profusely day and night, which caused him to wonder if he might have malaria. Even in these unbearable conditions, each person received only a small amount of water and a cup of thin rice gruel each day.

Sleep refused to come as he lay on the thin pad they issued him for a bed. As he lay there in a puddle of sweat and surrounded by pesky mosquitoes, every muscle in his body seemed to cry out with pain, and his mind raced beyond control: *I wonder how Keng is doing? If there has ever been a time in her life when she needed me, it is right now, and I cannot be there for her. She seemed to be so terribly weak, and she could hardly waddle around when I left. It is probably worse by now. These evil monsters really mean it when they say, "To kill you is no loss to us."*

For the first time since the soldiers had forced him onto Highway 6 as he left Phnom Penh, he allowed himself to think at length about Guek. *Perhaps she has escaped this hellish existence. I certainly hope so. I cannot help but wonder what message she had for me when she came to visit me in the prison.*

"God, please forgive me if I have been wrong in acting as a husband to Keng without knowing what has happened to Guek. If this chalad is my punishment for that, it certainly does seem excessive. Please forgive any sin I have committed and help me in this situation. Amen."

A Group Escape

As time dragged on and conditions worsened, SamSan established contact with a group of eight men who were planning an escape attempt. One of them—a former district governor in Cambodia—had a compass, and another had a crude map of the approximately one-hundred-kilometer path to Thailand and freedom. The group had only a very small supply of food consisting of a kilo or two of rice, a few small, dried fish, and some dried beef that came from a calf they had found dead.

SamSan had known people to lose fingers and toes or even to die after eating dried beef from an animal carcass, but he honestly believed he could not survive much longer in the hell he faced daily here on this chalad, and no end appeared in sight for that.

Although it meant completely ignoring his commitment to Keng's father and to Keng that he would look after her, he decided to take the risk and join this group. He had reached the conclusion that his life was now totally hopeless and pointless. Death could not be any worse than was his life in this circumstance, so he must take this chance and try to escape at any cost.

He justified his act because of Keng's advanced pregnancy. *She could not go with us even if she was in the camp with me*, he reasoned. *She will have to look after herself. Right now, I must do whatever I have to do to survive.*

Before sunrise the following morning, immediately after reporting to their work in the rice paddy, the nine men slipped out of sight and into the jungle. They often stumbled in their haste as they tried to follow the imagined trail heading northward toward Thailand. Finally, when they felt they were far enough away from the camp to make their discovery by the guards less likely, they fell into exhausted sleep. They assigned shifts so that one person always remained awake to serve as a lookout.

The first rays of dawn the next morning found the men pressing on in their journey, but SamSan had begun to have second thoughts. *I made a solemn promise to Lor Sieng on his death bed that I would look after his daughter when he and her mother were gone. As a Christian, my word is supposed to be my bond. Even though Keng and I are apart at this*

*time, there is some hope that I may rejoin her in the near future. I cannot
live this lie of running away. I must turn back.*

SamSan told the other eight men about his decision and began his
trek back toward the camp. He had only gone about 300 meters when
he heard loud crashing sounds in the jungle behind him. He quickly hid
in the bushes and helplessly watched the sickening scene that unfolded
in front of his eyes. A Khmer Rouge patrol had stumbled onto the rest
of his party, and the soldiers were using the heavy spokes from oxcart
wheels as clubs to beat each of the other eight men to death.

As soon as the Khmer Rouge patrol disappeared from the area,
SamSan made all haste in getting back to the work camp. As he
strolled nonchalantly into the work area about three hours late for
work, a gruff Khmer Rouge med confronted him and yelled, "Where
in the hell have you been, Ly Peing? We have been looking all over
the place for you."

"Me go in jungle look for mushrooms last might," SamSan said.
"Me get lost. Jungle scary place at night. Many strange noises."

"You get your butt back to work, and do not forget, you owe me
three hours of hard labor," said the irritated med as he shoved SamSan
toward the jobsite. "Mushrooms indeed, and in the dark at that."

Although he was given a severe lashing for his tardiness, SamSan
considered himself lucky to have survived that incident. He realized
that his decision to remain true to a commitment made to a dying man
had spared him a horrible death. "Thank You, God," he prayed silently.

Home Again

It took about a month after SamSan's aborted escape attempt for
the group on *chalad* to complete gathering the rice crop. His heart
beat wildly as he returned to his commune at Kom Pong K Dey. He
had beaten the *chalad*, and now he would rejoin Keng. However,
the couple's reunion had to be matter-of-fact because of the Khmer
Rouge restriction on any public display of emotion.

"It is wonderful to see you again, Keng, but you look so thin and pale," he said as he first laid eyes on her. "I believe you have lost at least a couple of kilograms while I was gone. You should be gaining weight when you are pregnant, not losing it. How are you feeling now?"

Keng replied dolefully and tearfully, "Oh, SamSan, it has been so hard without having you here with me. Every day at work I have felt dizzy and I have almost fainted again at least two more times. Somehow I have managed to get my work done every day, so I did not get into any kind of trouble with the cadre, but it has really been hard for me to carry on all by myself."

"Your being weak does not surprise me at all," SamSan said. "I feel certain you are anemic. These evil beasts say they 'want us to have children for the good of Angkar,' and then starve us to death. How can they expect a woman to carry a baby when they never give her enough to eat, never give her any food with protein, and they do not have any medical care?

"As soon as I can get some of my strength back, I will see what I can do about finding something you can eat that will give you some iron and protein. You need that kind of food if you are to build up your strength. You need some meat. Why do they fail to give us anything with iron and protein?"

A few days later, SamSan ignored the danger to his own life as he crept stealthily about the village after midnight for several consecutive nights looking for some source of protein and iron for Keng. He did not dare take one of the commune animals from its pen, because he knew that would cost the life of the keeper of that animal. However, he did examine several sleeping cows and water buffaloes to look for attached ticks and leeches, but he failed to find anything that would provide the nutrition Keng needed.

In desperation, he took off his clothes and immersed himself in the lake for several hours one night to allow its dreaded leeches to attach themselves to his body and feed for a while. When he came out of the water, he removed the ten leeches that had attached to his skin. These leeches had filled themselves with his blood until they had become slightly larger than the end of his thumb. He removed the leeches and prepared a soup with them, using a small amount of rice stolen from the village commander's pantry. He fed the hot soup to his wife in hopes it would give her enough strength to carry this pregnancy to term. Perhaps the soup did strengthen Keng to carry on with the pregnancy, but not as much as it strengthened her love and respect for her husband who had risked his own life and made such a sacrifice for her.

The village director seemed happy to have SamSan back in the community, and he resumed his policy of assigning his watchmaker to work at small tasks locally. However, from a number of statements he heard the official make, SamSan got the feeling that his benefactor lived under great pressure as village director and could possibly be in grave danger. Those statements led SamSan to wonder if the director was considering an attempt to escape to Thailand soon.

Reading between the lines of the village director's remarks made SamSan believe there had been some changes in the higher echelons of the Khmer Rouge, and they had expressed unhappiness with the achievements of the commune at Kom Pong K Dey. His benefactor had made no definite statement, but the young Cambodian assumed he would ask Keng and himself to join in an escape effort soon. Again, he wondered how much his village director actually knew about his background and how much of this information he had shared with others. More importantly, who, if anybody, had received that information about him? It worried him considerably, but he could do nothing about it.

A Child Is Born

Keng's pregnancy came to term and she went into labor, perhaps a couple of weeks prematurely—it was so hard to measure time in such circumstances. The village midwife assisted her as she brought a small baby boy into the world without as much as a glass of wine to ease the pain. Keng immediately put the baby to breast but, in her starved condition, she could not produce enough milk to nourish him. She and SamSan used a portion of their daily rice ration to make a white colored, rice-water solution that they fed to the baby several times a day. Many different members of the Khmer Rouge cadre blatantly ignored their pleas for milk for the infant, and the child died of starvation after fifteen days.

SamSan had a feeling of intense bitterness as he buried his baby in an unmarked grave: bitterness because of the Khmer Rouge's unfeeling refusal of food for his long-desired child. Bitterness because he could not mourn his loss since any sign of unhappiness would be viewed by the Khmer Rouge as rejection of Angkar and punishable by death. Bitterness because they had forcefully separated him from his legal wife and had never allowed him to search for her, and his list went on.

One day while SamSan still dealt with his bitterness, he carried out an assigned task in the village director's home. His boss feasted lustily and noisily from a heaping plate of fish on the table in front of him. He frequently threw a piece of the fish to his dog, as the animal stood at the director's feet begging. SamSan could hardly hold his tongue as his own severe hunger pangs seemed to grow much more intense each time the chubby dog waddled across the room to pick up a morsel of fish thrown by his master. However, he restrained his bitter spirit and simply laughed and patted the dog on his head until the two had become good friends. "Good boy," he said to the dog. "You fine-looking animal."

SamSan always carried a rice sack with him on the off chance he might find some food to put in it. A few days later, when he completed his workday in the village, he passed the director's home on his way back to his hovel. The village official's dog followed the hungry Cambodian down the narrow path that led to his residence, and SamSan made no effort to chase him away. When they got into an area where the brush grew quite thick on each side of his path and no one could see him, SamSan pulled the rice sack from his pocket and enticed the dog to come closer. He then squatted down as if to pet the animal and hurriedly put the sack over the dog.

Before the dog could yelp enough to attract attention, the young watchmaker had immersed the sack into the waters of a small canal that flowed beside the path. All movement and noise from the captured animal soon disappeared, and SamSan skinned the dog immediately and buried the telltale evidence in the jungle.

He and Keng shared their bounty with Kok Kuong and his family that night. After his first decent meal in weeks, SamSan swatted at an annoying mosquito and laughed heartily for the first time in ages. Then he rubbed his bulging belly and said, "I guess that will teach Mr. Village Director not to feed a dog that is already too fat in front of a really hungry man."

Privilege Lost

The Khmer Rouge action came swiftly and silently, and the unexpressed fears SamSan had sensed from the village director came to fruition. Headquarters called his friend and benefactor to a meeting, and he simply did not return. As rumors of his death spread quickly through the commune, SamSan could not help but think, *There goes my hope of getting some help in trying to get out of this madness. Was it just wishful thinking on my part that he might ask me to help him in an escape attempt, or did the director simply wait until it became too late to carry out his plan? I suppose I will never know.*

What will life be like in this hellish place now? And why did they have to make a change at just the time when I thought I had it worked out to the point where Keng and I could bear life here?

The new village director came on the scene with a flurry of action. He immediately put into effect the plan the previous director had told SamSan was in the works. With only one exception, the Khmer Rouge transferred all Chinese families from Kom Pong K Dey to other villages. This action separated SamSan from his dear friend, Kok Kuong, but it brought the community into line with the new rule for all communes. The Khmer Rouge hoped this action would lessen the chance for the resourceful Chinese citizens to organize any kind of opposition to their iron-fisted rule.

SamSan said to Keng, "To me, this seems a strange way to treat citizens who come from your closest ally." Nevertheless, he and Keng were among the families classified as Chinese who had to move to another commune.

As the couple trudged through the steamy jungle paths on their way to Tar Nguon, their new village about eleven kilometers southeast from Kom Pong K Dey, they could almost feel the constant watchful eyes of the Khmer Rouge cadre. Certainly, there was no clear chance for them to turn aside and try to escape on this trip. SamSan had personally witnessed the horror of a failed escape attempt. Furthermore, there had been no opportunity to prepare for such a venture.

"I wonder what life will be like in our new community," said Keng.

"It could not be any worse than it has been up until now," SamSan replied. "After all, you have had to bury your father and your mother as well as your baby. The only thing we have left now is one another, and the important thing is just to survive. Surely the world will not allow this holocaust to go on much longer.

"Fortunately, I have two watches left. The one I used in Kom Pong K Dey seemed to have been effective in buying us favor with the leader in that camp. Our plan right now still has to be simply to stay alive. After that, we can think about buying a little political favor with our watches; but we have no choice except to continue to handle each situation as it comes up until God delivers us from this horrible mess."

NEW COMMUNE—
NEW PROBLEMS

Jar Nguon, Cambodia—
Late Fall? 1978

When SamSan and Keng arrived at their new commune, he immediately sought out the village head. "Sir, me Ly Peing," he said, "but most meds call me Chinese Ly. This is wife, Muoy Keng. In Kom Pong K Dey, me do much odd jobs for village director. Me watchmaker and general repairman for commune. Me fix almost anything. Wife is seamstress. She make good clothes for all leaders."

"We bring you good present," SamSan continued as he handed the next to the last of his watches to the village director. "Is one Titony watch. Is very fine watch from Switzerland for high person. Me not high person, me not wear. You high person, you wear."

The new village director seemed happy to have a good watch. "That is very thoughtful of you, Chinese Ly, and yes, a man in my position does need a fine watch. It is also good to have a watchmaker in town since many of my people have trouble keeping their appointments on time. They always blame their watches. We will put you in a place where your talents can benefit our commune the most."

He assigned SamSan to duties similar to those he had performed in Kom Pong K Dey, mostly within the central commune, and he made Keng the town seamstress. SamSan felt much more comfortable in this location because he felt certain the village director had no knowledge of his education and his past. In Kom Pong K Dey, there had always been that uneasy feeling that the head of the village knew more about his watchmaker's background than he ever allowed anyone to know.

However, he still had to be careful. In the Khmer Rouge system, one could never get too comfortable. Every person you met held the possibility of being a spy for Angkar, and every action or word could possibly be a life-or-death matter. He did his assigned job and kept his mouth shut unless someone addressed him directly.

He had only been in this commune a few days when the village director sent the local military commander to see him. The commander brought his broken watch, a cheap Chinese product. The official looked on expectantly as SamSan removed the back from the timepiece. His facial expression turned quizzical as the watchmaker took one look and exclaimed, "Oh my goodness."

"What is wrong with it?" asked the Khmer Rouge commander.

"Mainspring broke," SamSan said. "No can fix watch even if had new parts."

"What can we do about it, then?" asked the military commander. "I need a good watch so I can keep up with my appointments, and there is no place where a person can buy one in Cambodia now."

SamSan knew that a military commander had enough authority to commandeer a watch from most anyone in the country, and he thought quickly. *I like this man. Taking a watch from someone else is not his first thought, although he has the power to do that. This man wields more life and death power than even the village director does, and this is my best chance to get on his good side. Here is the best place to spend my last watch.*

"Well, Med," he said in a serious tone of voice, "Me no can fix your watch but me need spare parts. Me swap with you–new watch for broken one. Is one Omsga watch. Is very fine watch from Switzerland made for high person. Me not high person, me not wear. You high person, you wear watch.

"You no need wind this watch. It wind self like magic when you move. You man of action and move a lot. If you no wind, no break mainspring like on other watch." He made a deep bow and smiled as he presented his gift to the military commander.

The Khmer Rouge officer surprisingly returned SamSan's deep bow and uttered an unthinkable "Thank you." SamSan smiled a knowing smile.

As the two saw one another in going about their duties in the commune, the military commander began to greet SamSan with, "Hello, Chinese Ly," a title that SamSan enjoyed even more now because the commander spoke it in a tone that sounded very pleasant. In those days, pleasantries had become a rare occurrence.

SamSan continued to perform his menial duties around the commune graciously and well. He constantly reminded himself about how much better his life seemed when he was doing these small tasks than it had been when he had to go on *chalad*.

When the local rice crop matured ready for harvest, the commune pressed him into duty for a few days to help with gathering the rice. As he worked in the rice paddy, his mind traveled back to his childhood days when Mrs. Allison taught him the religious song, "Bringing in the Sheaves." He remembered the hand motions she had taught him and noticed that they were quite similar to those his hands and arms were making as he reaped the grain heads in the rice paddy. How he cherished those memories and relished the feeling they brought to him in the middle of this time of dark desperation.

As he continued his repetitive, boring, and tiresome labor in the rice paddy, he momentarily forgot about his troubles as the words and tune of that song raced silently through his mind. The working motions of his hands kept perfect time with the melody he could hear so clearly in his head. In his reliving of those joyful moments from his youth, he apparently lost himself in the moment, and his silent singing unconsciously translated into audible song:

Sowing in the morning,
Sowing seeds of kindness,
Sowing in the noontide and the dewy eve.
Waiting for the harvest and the time of reaping,
We shall come rejoicing bringing in the sheaves.

A couple of days later, he wondered what was the occasion when the military commander showed up at his work site and said, "Chinese Ly, I want you to come with me." He was unaware that someone had heard him singing and had reported him to the village authorities for that illegal act.

"We not through with rice gathering, Med. Do you want me leave here?" SamSan asked.

"Yes," the military commander responded, "We need to go right away. The other workers will finish the rice harvest."

"Where going?" said SamSan.

"You will find that out soon enough," said the military commander as he got aboard his motorcycle and motioned for SamSan to sit behind him.

The roar of the motorcycle engine and the whistle of the wind as it whizzed past his unhelmeted ears made it impossible for SamSan to carry on any conversation or ask any further questions. He had seen Khmer Rouge officials take many other people on such motorcycle rides, but he could not remember seeing a single one of them return to the village.

This is the end, he thought.

Then his thoughts turned to Keng, *I wish the commander had given me time to say good-bye to her before I left. I am sure I will not be coming back from this ride.*

Throughout the entire two-hour ride, he prayed and his whole life flashed before him as he made his final peace with God. "God, I am ready for whatever happens now, amen." He breathed the final words of what he thought would be his final prayer.

When the motorcycle eventually pulled up at its destination, SamSan's heart sickened as he realized the commander had brought him to a prison. *I have never known the Khmer Rouge to imprison anybody*, he thought. *Displeasing them always brings swift death.*

Then he realized it was not a political prison. This was a place where they did short-time incarcerations of Khmer Rouge soldiers who had failed to please their commanding officers.

He could feel the color drain even further from his face when he saw a group of pretty, young Cambodian girls and recognized that a long vine impaled through the left hand of each girl chained them one to another. It sickened him. His escort explained that these girls would become the property of Khmer Rouge officials and would produce babies for Angkar to rear.

He then led SamSan into an administrative room attached to the prison where the Khmer Rouge had assembled a tribunal. As the bailiff called for another case, SamSan watched the procedure with rapt attention.

"What is the charge against this man?" asked the head judge.

"He is charged with being asleep when he should have been working," the bailiff replied.

"But I was sick and I had simply fainted. I was not asleep," the prisoner objected.

"Take him away and kill him," roared the head of the tribunal. "Anyone who will not work is not worthy to breathe the air of Angkar."

"Next case!" yelled the bailiff.

The military commander led SamSan to the platform where he stood unsteadily, directly in front of the tribunal judge.

"And what is the charge against this man?" asked the tribunal judge in a loud and belligerent voice.

"He is charged with singing a foreign song when he was at work," the military commander responded in his equally loud military voice that SamSan had never heard him employ.

"Oh no no no," SamSan responded impulsively, not realizing that he was supposed to remain silent. "It is not foreign song. It is Chinese song. It is song about reaping harvest, and I was happy, reaping for Angkar."

"And what are the words to this song?" the leader of the tribunal leaned forward as if to confront SamSan.

"Oh, they very good words for workers, sir," SamSan seemed emboldened as he replied, "because they keep spirits high, and the tune gives good rhythm to do their work."

SamSan cleared his throat and began to sing in the Khmer language in a loud baritone voice:

> "Sowing in the morning,
> Sowing seeds for Angkar,
> Sowing in the noontide and the dewy eve.
> Waiting for the harvest and the time of reaping
> We shall come rejoicing bringing in the sheaves."

"Oh, that is very good," exclaimed the head of the tribunal. "Med, take this man back home and have him teach this song to all of the other meds. It should be a great help to us in gathering our harvests. Case dismissed."

On the ride back to their commune, SamSan huddled close behind the military commander to shield himself as much as possible from the cold evening wind that raced by. He breathed another sigh of relief as he silently prayed, "God, I do not really believe it hurt anything to change just two words in the song. Instead of saying 'of kindness,' I said 'for Angkar'—but it did save my life. After all, Your name is never mentioned in the original version of the song, so I did not exclude You.

"I am sorry if You thought of it as a small lie, but I am certainly grateful the idea came into my head when it did. Otherwise, I would be a dead man right now. By the way, was it really You that gave me the idea in the first place? Amen."

When SamSan and the military commander got back to the village, both of them had to go back to business as usual. The young Cambodian stood completely aware of the debt of gratitude he owed the military commander who could have killed him on the spot. He knew the commander had total authority of life and death over every member of the commune and was not required to take anyone before any sort of tribunal. He owed his life to that med.

The realization that he had no more watches he could use to buy any further favor with Khmer Rouge officials loomed heavily on SamSan's mind. It meant that he must keep up his guard even more consciously and more constantly.

The next few months proved to be routine months of not enough food and many daily hours of backbreaking work. Both SamSan and Keng had become hardened to this exceedingly harsh existence, and he had become especially adept at his "midnight requisitions," sometimes not using cautionary measures. By applying every ounce of their wit and energy, the couple managed to continue to survive.

When the wet season of 1978 ended, SamSan noted that the number of Khmer Rouge soldiers who were savagely driving the slave laborers to produce more with less material seemed to be smaller than it had been before. Then he began to hear rumors that the Vietnamese Army was building up their forces on their border with Cambodia. Those rumors soon became a reality as the Vietnamese launched a massive military offensive to take over Cambodia.

Rumor had it that the horrendous treatment of its "New citizens" by the Communist Party of Cambodia had given communist rule everywhere a bad name. The Communist rulers of Vietnam had apparently made a decision and were determined to end the fiasco in Cambodia. The Vietnamese felt certain the enslaved masses would not rise up and fight against their invading army, no matter how much Cambodians had previously hated the Vietnamese. In fact, they fully expected those masses to rise up against their stone-fisted slave-masters and join them if the opportunity arose.

Vietnamese soldiers attacked in wave after massive wave with great air support and soon overwhelmed the less well supplied Khmer Rouge forces by their sheer power. Many small, rag-tag and disorganized groups of Khmer Rouge fled into the jungles, while some of them joined with the floods of refugees going into Thailand. Some of these forces hoped to set up bases of resistance across the Thai border, from which they could attempt to retake their homeland.

On January 7, 1979, the Pol Pot regime fell. Deliverance had finally come for SamSan and Keng and the other oppressed masses.

DELIVERANCE—BUT HIS FAMILY IS LOST

Siem Riep Province, Cambodia—January 1979

Change came rapidly with the change of governments. The Khmer Rouge had kept all of the country's rice in grain storage facilities and used most of that grain to buy arms from China. In the meantime, many of their citizens literally starved to death. The new Vietnamese-controlled government opened those facilities and began to distribute rice in generous amounts to every family. They removed all travel restrictions and allowed husbands and wives to reunite if they could find one another. Families were encouraged to return to their original homes, though they provided no transportation and many of the homes had been destroyed.

SamSan thought the new regime had intentionally designed their freedom of movement policy to encourage citizens to become refugees. *After all,* he reasoned, *when someone leaves the country, the Vietnamese have one less mouth to feed.*

Myriads of refugees suddenly took to the highways. Some headed for Thailand, but even more tried to return home and rebuild their shattered lives. Confusion reigned on the highways again, but not the massive frightened confusion that had reigned during the Khmer Rouge takeover.

The new government opened up the borders of Cambodia to international inspection teams. They invited special attention to the region where they had found so many mass graves that the world had named the area "The Killing Fields." SamSan believed the reason for that open policy was to sway world opinion. They wanted to spread throughout the world the innumerable tales of horror these refugees had experienced because they believed those stories would justify their invasion of Cambodia in the eyes of the world. "We came to rescue you, not to occupy your land" became their often-repeated theme to the Cambodian people.

SamSan wanted to join the exodus from Cambodia right away, but Keng expressed great fears about such a move.

"We do not have a map," she said, "and we do not have nearly enough supplies to last us on that long trip through the jungle. In addition, I have heard a number of reports about Khmer Rouge bands hanging out in the jungle. People say they support themselves by terrorizing and robbing groups of refugees and that they have even taken some of them as captive slave laborers. I do not want to take any chance of ever becoming a slave laborer again."

Then she added the clincher to her argument. "And do you believe it is a good time for us to take on a trip like that while I am pregnant?"

"While you are what?"

"While I am pregnant," Keng confirmed. "I had not told you before now because I did not want you to worry."

SamSan felt a flurry of mixed emotions as he replied, "Well, that certainly does make a difference. It means we will need to make a decision quickly about where we will live, and I must find something to do to make a living for my family right away.

"Let me see," he thought aloud, "it does not make any sense for us to go back to Phnom Penh. We only had a rented apartment there, and we have no kinfolks or property there any more to tie us to the city. Furthermore, the royal family is out of power, so I do not have any political pull. I have no assurance that I could find a job there. The same things seem to be true about Battambang, unless some of my family has survived, so we should either stay right here or we go to America."

"I vote to stay right here," Keng replied without hesitation.

"You may be right, Keng," SamSan replied, " but we will have to find a way to support ourselves. The leaders in the new government in Siem Riep Province do not know yet that I speak several languages. They are certain to need a large number of interpreters, and you know there are not many of us left who can do that. Maybe our best bet is for us to stay right here for the time being, apply for work as an interpreter, and see what happens. However, I sure do hate the idea of having to continue living under any kind of communist rule. And I hate the idea of having to work with and for a communist government even worse."

No longer feeling the need to hide his linguistic abilities, SamSan boldly strode into the Siem Riep Province headquarters to report to the local officials and, for the first time in four years, he spoke in Vietnamese. Astounded that they had a survivor who spoke ten languages, they opened up their arms to him and immediately absorbed him into their system. He served as a translator in many situations where the language barrier would have otherwise created problems. Time no longer stood still for this survivor. His world had begun to function again.

The more exposure they had to SamSan's translation skills, the more the local Vietnamese authorities became excited about him and his potential in their system. According to their talk, they were laying out a bright future for him in their new government structure. Their first step was to send him to study at a new school of politics recently opened near Siem Riep. There was talk about sending him to Moscow for training to become an embassy official for the new Democratic Republic of Cambodia. In the meantime, they appointed him Deputy Director and Official Postmaster for Siem

Riep Province. With these appointments, they provided housing for him in one of the better structures in Siem Riep.

SamSan's governmental appointments at that particular moment were only titles on paper. No vestige of an organized postal service existed at that moment, nor had there been even so much as a job description written for the Deputy Director of a province at this early stage in the new government. SamSan could not function in either of his appointed positions at that time, and he felt any attempt to do so would waste his time and that of others. He decided to use this special gift of time off with pay to mount a search for Guek and to look for his parents.

"Do not be too long," said Keng.

A Second Search for Guek

He loaded his bicycle onto a Soviet-made Vietnamese army truck and began a three-day and two-night journey to the Battambang area, a distance of about one hundred seventy kilometers. After the truck deposited him in Battambang, he rode his bicycle another seventy-plus kilometers to the small village of Mong Russei, where Guek's parents had lived. To his dismay, he found the old family home destroyed, and he could not locate a single surviving member of her family.

After making many inquiries in all of the surrounding houses, he found a former neighbor who had been in the same commune with Guek for a short time. "Can you tell me anything about my wife? Her name is Nai Guek, and she grew up in this neighborhood," he said.

"Yes, yes, I know the person you are talking about. Now let me see—the Khmer Rouge killed her about two or three years ago," responded the neighbor. "They tell me she had a baby—"

"She what?" SamSan shouted.

"I said she had a baby a few months after the Khmer Rouge took over Cambodia," the neighbor continued." She and her husband were separated when the Khmer Rouge took over, as a whole lot of other families were. They tell me he did not even know she was pregnant when she came back here, but some folks said—"

"I know, I know," said SamSan. "I am that husband and the Cambodian army was holding me in prison—"

"Well, anyhow, she did have a baby. A boy, I believe," the neighbor continued, seemingly oblivious to SamSan's remarks. "And when he was about a year old, he got sick. His mama went to the Khmer Rouge and asked them for some medicine to treat his fever. They did not believe in any kind of Western medicine, and the nurse refused to give her anything.

"Guek…you say she was your wife, do you?" he said disdainfully. "Well, anyhow she spotted a packet of aspirin on a table and slipped them into her pocket. The Khmer Rouge saw her when she took the medicine, and they killed her on the spot. I believe the person who told me about it said they hit her in the head with either a hoe or an axe."

"It makes me sick to think of it, she was so fragile, those dirty–" SamSan broke off. "Yes, she was my wife, but I most certainly did not desert her, if that is what you are thinking."

"A few months before Phnom Penh fell, the Cambodian government arrested me on false charges. We had been trying to have a baby for the full six years we had been married, and she had not given any indication at all that she was pregnant before my arrest. She had not missed a period when they dragged me away and threw me in jail.

"Somebody said she had come by the prison where I was held to try to see me. They said she had some kind of a family message for me, but they did not know what the message was. Anyhow, the prison officials would not let her visit me, and they were unkind to her. I figure she got frightened and came back home, but I could only guess about what the message was she wanted to give me. I did wonder if she might finally be pregnant after all those years of trying.

"And now, I know the truth," he blinked back a tear. "Guek had a baby, and it was a boy…" his voice trailed off.

"I tried to come to Battambang to look for her when the Khmer Rouge released me from prison, but the soldiers threatened to kill me if I did not take the Siem Riep highway from Phnom Penh." SamSan's voice grew louder and his words came faster as he changed the subject almost in mid-sentence.

"But please tell me everything you know about my baby. Do you know if he is still alive and who is taking care of him? Can you tell me where I can find him? Or, better still, can you take me to him? I need to find my son."

"Not so fast, my friend," said the neighbor. "I understand that you want to find your son, and I want to help you, but slow down. My source—and I cannot remember who it was that told me—said that a few months after Guek was killed, her brother, Nai Muoy, took the baby and tried to escape from Cambodia. That was about a year and a half ago, and nobody has heard anything from either of them since that time, so we have assumed that both of them are dead.

"You know how it is; nobody knows anything for certain about anything in Cambodia anymore. Some mighty strange things have happened here in the past four years. You must not give up hope for your son."

"Thank you, my friend, you have been a great help to me," SamSan said. His mind raced with a plethora of emotions as he turned to go. His tears flowed freely as he grieved the loss of Guek and his son.

I really did love Guek, and she loved me, he thought. *We had six good years together, and I was always true to her.* Yet he felt a certain degree of relief at the assurance he was not technically guilty of bigamy. *I believed that Guek was probably dead before Keng and I started being intimate*, he reasoned. *And Keng and I did not get into that situation by choice either. I believe the hand of God brought us together, but if I am wrong, I believe He has forgiven me, .*

I have such terribly mixed feelings about my son, he mused. *On the one hand, I am happy to know he was born, but I am heartbroken that he is missing and probably dead. But, starting right now, I shall look for him until I either find him or I know exactly what has happened to him.*

A Search for Family

Bewildered by the knowledge that the Khmer Rouge had killed Guek and that his son was missing, SamSan rode his bicycle back to Battambang, where he planned to search for his adoptive parents. In the old neighborhood, he found a man and his wife who had returned to their home after having spent some time in the same commune with his parents.

After exchanging greetings, he asked them, "Can you tell me anything about my father or my mother? Do you know if either of them is still alive? I have heard nothing from them for the past four years. The Khmer Rouge held me in the labor commune in Siem Riep province, and I could not know where they held them. I need to know if they are still alive and where they are now. Do you have any knowledge of what has happened to them?"

"Just one question at a time, young man," the old man answered quickly, "Yes, I can tell you about your father, but I hate to be the bearer of bad news. Your father starved to death nearly four years ago, shortly after they forced us to go to the fields to work. He had been on *chalad* for possibly as much as six weeks when it happened. Those of us who were with him at the time thought he was mighty lucky to be out of his misery that soon. We were all jealous because he looked to be at perfect peace as he laid there a corpse. The rest of us had to continue our suffering for nearly four more years."

His wife then chimed in. "And I was with your mother when she died. We were gathering rice in a rice paddy along with her two grand-daughters—you know Marilyn's two little girls, Socheat and Malis—and a bunch of other women. Su Ho apparently decided she could not take the hard work and abuse any longer, so she started singing her favorite song, I believe it is called 'When We All Get to Heaven.'

"Her granddaughters warned her again and again, 'Granny, you had better hush that singing. The soldiers will come and kill you if you keep it up.'

"But your mama would not hush. You know how determined Su Ho could be when she made up her mind to do something. She did it no matter what anybody else had to say or what they thought."

The neighbor wiped a tear from her eye and continued, "She just kept on singing 'When We All Get to Heaven' until one of the Khmer Rouge cadre came and hit her in the head with a hoe or something. I guess that might be a good way for a Christian to leave this world, but it is not for me."

"What about Marilyn's girls? What happened to them?" SamSan asked.

"I understand that the younger one, Malis, was killed, but I do not know how she died. And they tell me that Socheat, the oldest one, is in Thailand as a refugee," the old woman said.

The dismal news about the loss of so many of his family members made the long bicycle ride to Siem Riep seem much longer. SamSan became even more determined to get out of his country and go to America.

His Family Established

As soon as her husband returned to their home, Keng asked him excitedly, "What did you find out about Guek and the rest of your family?"

"Guek had a baby, and—"

"She what?"

"Yes, she had a baby." A tear rolled down his cheek and his lip quivered. "But the baby got sick when he was about a year old. She stole some aspirin to treat his fever, and the Khmer Rouge killed her. The dirty scoundrels caught her with the aspirin and killed her on the spot.

"The neighbors say the baby is probably dead too, because Guek's brother, Muoy, took him to try to go to Thailand eighteen months ago, and no one has heard from either of them since.

"I also found out that Mother and Daddy are dead and that Marilyn's oldest daughter got killed, but I do not know how. The other one, Socheat, may be in Thailand as a refugee.

"Basically, that is it in a nutshell: I have no family left in Battambang, and I could not find any of Guek's family either." Keng held SamSan close to her until he could control his tears and quit his sobbing.

He had never felt any real guilt about his relationship with Keng, only a mild uneasiness. However, now that he was certain he could not return to Guek, he felt totally free to be a husband to Keng. A few weeks later, she presented him with a healthy son, and they named him David, after the biblical king.

The End is in Sight

Siem Riep, Cambodia—
Late October 1979

As deputy village director and postmaster of Siem Riep, SamSan
lived in a government provided house on the main thoroughfare in
town. From this vantage point, he saw most of the transients who
passed through the town. One day a group of nine haggard, hungry,
and exhausted refugees came into his village headed in the opposite direction from most travelers. Thailand had forcibly expelled
them from their country, and they were on their way back home to
Battambang, SamSan's hometown.

The group had slipped out of Cambodia a few weeks earlier and
sought shelter in a temporary refugee camp in Thailand. After about
two weeks in this camp, the Thai government sent soldiers to threaten
them and rough them up. A few nights later, a stream of busses pulled
up to the refugee camp, and Thai soldiers forced hundreds of refugees, including their group, onto them. The busses drove to the Thai
border with Cambodia, where the soldiers had the passengers disem-
bark, then fired rifles over the heads of the frightened refuges while
instructing them to go home or be killed. A Thai bullet killed at least
one person who attempted to turn back into Thailand.

With no compass and no map for the trail they had to follow, and
with precious little food and supplies, the group had spent several
days of wandering, lost in the dense jungle that covered the moun-

tains. One young man in their group had died, possibly from eating poison fruit or mushrooms.

When SamSan saw the disheveled group, they appeared very near to the end of their endurance. One of the women in the group recognized SamSan and said in a very loud voice, "I know you. You grew up in Battambang. Your mama and my mama used to be best friends, and your mama tried to arrange for you to marry my sister, Lor Noy. I am Lor Tang, Noy's younger sister."

"You cannot be," SamSan said with a laugh.

"The reason you do not recognize me is because I was quite young then, and you only had eyes for Noy at that time." Tang joined in the laughter.

"Oh my goodness," SamSan exclaimed. "I can see the resemblance now. You do look a lot like Noy. How do you come to be in Siem Riep?"

"It is a long story, if you want to hear it," Tang replied.

"By all means," he said as he settled in his chair.

"I had worked hard all my life," Tang began, "and had just begun to have a few of the nicer things, when the Khmer Rouge took over. I managed to hide most of my treasures from their soldiers, because they were not very smart. Now that the Vietnamese have taken over, they are a lot smarter, but they are Communists just the same. I felt sure that they would find out about the things I have hidden away very soon, and they would want to take them away from me. Of course, they would say, 'It is for the good of the people'—but you and I know what people it would be good for."

"I certainly do," SamSan grinned as he spoke. "I have noticed how well the leaders live while the peasants do all the work and still get poorer all the time."

"A lot of my family felt the same way I did," Tang continued. "They did not want to live under communism either, so we got together, and ten of us decided we would go to Thailand. Shortly after we crossed the border into Thailand, we settled in with a large group of refugees, but we had to make our own makeshift camp. There were not any sanitary facilities and very little water for us in that place and it had no organization at all. Thai soldiers raped a number of women and robbed many refugees. The Thai police did not care and would not do a thing about it. It was awful."

"I am surprised to hear that," SamSan said. "My experience with the Thai people has always been very good. I have found them to be a very gentle people."

"Some of the Thai people were kind to us, but the Thai soldiers and a few of the Thai people treated us like we were lower than dirt. After about two weeks, the government sent a bunch of busses to pick us up, and the soldiers threatened us the same way the Khmer Rouge used to do. They herded us like cattle into those busses and carried us far across the country to the most mountainous part of the border between Thailand and Cambodia. You know the area. It is where the Khmer Rouge planted so many land mines so they would not have to patrol it."

SamSan shook his head as he replied, "Yes, I have heard about the area, but I have never been there."

"They did not really want us to go home. They wanted us to die and they thought this was a good way to kill us. The trail we had followed when we went into Thailand was pretty level and seemed to be clear of land mines, and it was much closer to the camp where we had been staying." A tear trickled down Tang's cheek and she could not continue.

Tang's teenage male cousin, Samsien, took over her story. "We saw several people who fell and broke their limbs," he continued, "and even more who stepped on land mines and were killed or maimed. There was one old woman who could not walk and her two daughters tried to carry her on a stretcher. The mountain was so steep, the woman kept falling off the stretcher and knocking her daughters down. They finally decided it was impossible to carry their mother over that terrain, and they left her there to die.

"To lessen the chance of stepping on a land mine, we all lined up like human dominoes. You put one hand on the person in front of you so you could step where that person had shown it was clear. The person that led the line was usually a Muslim, because they believe everyone has a set time to die and there are no accidental deaths, so they were not afraid. With the steep mountain and the land mines, we could only travel about one kilometer a day."

"No wonder you look so worn out," SamSan remarked.

"My cousin, who was just a little younger than me, must have eaten something poisonous. We had just come down out of the mountains when he started having convulsions, and I could not hold him down. I watched him die and could not do a thing about it. I had never actually seen anyone die before that. It was terrible," Samsien shuddered as he left off speaking.

Tang picked up the tale again. "When we finally got out of the mountains, the trails had almost no markings. Without a map, we spent a lot of time wandering lost in the jungle. Now we are trying to get back to Battambang so we can get more supplies and try again. We hear that the United Nations has some camps that are organized, and many folks are getting out. We definitely do not want to live under communism."

"Would you like to stay with us for a few days until you regain your strength?" SamSan asked. "We can find places for you to sleep and you can bring me up to date on the news from Battambang."

"Oh, that sounds wonderful," Tang replied.

SamSan's Dream

SamSan went to bed that night torn between two huge desires. The desire he had always had to "be somebody" seemed to lie at his fingertips. The new regional government had appointed him to a prominent office in their system and there been many allusions to his possible advancement to high places in the new government of Cambodia. However, he hated every experience he ever had with communism, and his other lifelong desire had been to go to America. In his heart of hearts, he knew he could never again be happy in Cambodia.

His dream during that night of fitful sleep seemed more real than any dream he had ever had. In it, he was starting out on a journey to America, and many different problems kept popping up to block his way. A beautiful bright light suddenly appeared on the horizon, and when he followed that light, it led him to a huge American flag. He felt assured that this was a promise from God that his escape to America would be successful, although there might be many difficulties. His immediate response was that he would be happy to face whatever difficulties his dream predicted for a chance at freedom for himself and his family.

When he told Keng about his dream the following morning, she agreed to go with him wherever he went. Later that day, while the children played outside, he approached the adults in the group from Battambang with his idea.

"Why do you need to go back to Battambang before you try to escape again?" he asked. "Why not stay here for a while to get some rest and gather supplies? It will save you over three hundred kilometers of travel, and everything you need for another escape attempt is available right here in Siem Riep."

A Family Created

"Keng and I have had a long talk this morning and would like to join you if you will allow us to come. The fact that you have already learned so much by crossing the border once should help us a great deal. I also believe my ability to speak Thai will make it easier for us when we get to Thailand. Then, my connections to the American military and my knowledge of English should help us get on to America."

Among the nine returning refugees, only two chose to continue back to Battambang and accept their life under communist rule. After two more days of rest, that pair headed for home. The other four adults and three children were eager to accept SamSan's proposal and get ready for another attempt to gain their freedom.

The new group of ten made an inventory of their supplies and a list of things they would need. They planned the route they would travel to the border and agreed on the logistics of their escape. Someone in the group had heard that families were never separated after they got to a refugee camp, and they all agreed they wanted to stay together at least until they reached their destination in America. Therefore, Keng claimed Tang as her sister, and both of them claimed Lan to be their aunt. When someone suggested that Lan's young age made that relationship appear unlikely, they simply added ten years to her actual age.

SamSan continued to give due diligence to his politically appointed offices during the time when plans were being formulated for their escape. He knew that the Vietnamese did not mind if an ordinary citizen left the country, but common sense told him the rules would be entirely different if an appointed official were to leave. He dared not take any action that might give anyone cause to suspect his plan to defect.

He asked Keng to sell a few of the rings he had gotten in Phnom Penh, but he did not personally make any of the sales or make any large purchases of supplies. The other members of the escape team purchased most of the needed supplies so as not to attract any attention to him and his plan. He scheduled the group's departure for a day when his assignment called for him to be out of his office. After agreeing that nothing could be worse than their certain fate if they stayed in Cambodia—a life under communist rule—the determined group prepared to face the unknown.

The Big Gamble

SamSan arranged to rent a horse-drawn cart to carry some of the women and children to the nameless, small community on the edge of the jungle near Phumi Thmei, only a few kilometers from Siem Riep. He reasoned that this façade would make their departure appear as if he were merely taking his visitors on a holiday jaunt. The cart also gave him a place to hide most of the supplies for their journey from the eyes of nosey neighbors and those ever-present Vietnamese watchdogs.

From this small village, the group entered the jungle for their adventure in early November of 1979. Carrying all of their belongings on their backs or strapped to three bicycles, the six adults and four children began their perilous journey toward their dream of freedom.

Samsien, Tang, and SamSan served as advance scouts, checking out every area of the jungle before the main group ventured into it. Pong stayed in camp with the remaining women and children until the advance group returned to give the okay for proceeding to the next objective. At times their map proved to be very sketchy and the trail markings confusing. When this was the case, the compass became their mainstay to guide their journey.

SamSan was eager to get to America, and it seemed to him that each kilometer of progress came at a snail's pace and with more than the expected amount of difficulty. However, his dream had predicted many problems. They had to investigate every noise and each slight movement in the jungle, since it could possibly be a Vietnamese patrol or, worse still, a patrol from the Khmer Rouge. He remembered Keng's warning that some of the Khmer Rouge bands who had retreated into the jungle obtained most of their needed supplies by robbing refugees.

He felt assured that the Vietnamese Army would have patrols out looking for their appointed official as soon as his superiors realized he was gone. He knew they would be very unhappy with a deputy village director who had abandoned his post, and he felt equally certain they would put him to death if they should catch him. At the very best, he expected he would spend several years rotting away in their prisons. Every person the group met posed a potential life-threatening danger, and each village loomed as a possible prison.

As the group slowly made their way through the jungle, they heard rifle fire almost every day, and one day a bullet struck a tree very close to their location. Whenever they heard gunfire, the group always reacted as if the shots were fired at them. They always took cover for an hour or so before they investigated the source of the bullet or entertained any thought of venturing further.

Each night when the freedom seekers made camp, the children gathered wood for the campfire while one of the adults went into the nearest village to get a hot coal to kindle a fire and to buy perishable goods they needed for their meal. In the meanwhile, Pong strung all of their unused pots and pans on strings around the camp as noise-makers to warn of any intruders.

On the second night of their journey, Pong's alarm system sounded, and he grabbed a machete to chase away the would-be robber. The children could not help but giggle later as they recalled the sight of a man as small as Pong wielding his huge weapon and dashing into the darkness to save their precious supplies from the thief.

Almost every day of their journey, the advance scouts endured the fearsome and distracting sight of one or more decaying corpses lying in the jungle. They always guided the group far around those areas where death had occurred to protect the children from the spectacle and the odor. They also feared the possibility of land mines planted about the body or of robbers lying in wait for unsuspecting travelers who stopped to gawk.

About a week into their journey, the group heard the unmistakable hum of a military vehicle's engine and ran quickly for cover. Six or eight Vietnamese soldiers on patrol through the jungle in a Russian-built truck passed within a hundred meters of the huddled travelers. SamSan could understand a few words of their conversation. Was it his imagination, or did he really hear them mention the village director who had defected from Siem Riep?

The jungle proved as hard on their equipment as it was on the travelers. By the end of their journey, they had abandoned one of the bicycles, and most of their shoes had failed and had to be discarded. The sharp blades of jungle grass and the penetration points of multiple thorns left their bare feet bleeding and terribly painful. This slowed their travel even further.

Finally, after about three weeks of hardship, and with most of their supplies exhausted, the weary group reached the confines of Refugee Camp 007. Their early sense of elation soon turned to deep despair when they learned that they had not crossed the border into Thailand. Furthermore, they heard that Thailand had decreed they would not accept any more refugees. Every report they heard from both the refugees and camp officials included the fact that no refugee from that camp had made the trip to freedom across the Thai border in the past two weeks.

Trapped in Camp 007
Near the Thai border in
Cambodia—Late November 1979

SamSan had burned all of his bridges behind him and could not turn back. He had no question as to what his fate would be if he had to return to Siem Riep. In spite of the fact that their situation appeared hopeless, he could not give up his dream without pulling every possible string to overcome the legal red tape. After all, his dream had warned him that his group would face many problems, and he tried to cling doggedly to the assurance he had felt after that dream. As the spokesman for his group, the time had come for him to be aggressive. However, as he tried to reason with the reception clerk at the camp, his spirits fell even lower.

"I am sorry, sir," said the emotionless clerk, "but the country of Thailand is no longer accepting refugees from the country of Cambodia."

SamSan's dark brown eyes were penetrating as he stared in disbelief at the receiving clerk. "I suppose you realize you have just sealed my death warrant," he said. "That decision makes me a man without a country."

"I am very sorry if that is so, sir," said the clerk as he repeated his matter-of-fact explanation. "But the fact remains that the country of Thailand is a sovereign nation and has made the decision to no longer accept any refugees from the country of Cambodia. The function of Camp 007 is to register your group and—"

"Yes, but I, and possibly everyone in my group, will most likely be killed if we go back to Cambodia now. I am a marked man. The Khmer Rouge and the Vietnamese factions there would both like to kill me. You see, I worked in the past with American soldiers in Vietnam and Cambodia, so the Khmer Rouge would love to see me dead, and the new Vietnamese government had assigned me to a post as a deputy director of a Cambodian province. I abandoned that post to come here. So both the Khmer Rouge and the so-called legitimate government of Cambodia will be searching for me. If we go back, they will probably not stop with killing just me."

"I totally understand your concern, Mr. Ouch, and every other refugee I have seen also feels the same. He is afraid he will be killed if he goes back home. But—"

"I...I am not, as you say, 'every other refugee,'" SamSan stammered a bit as he pulled out his comb to try to straighten his hopelessly disheveled black hair. "In fact, they have already tried to kill me. If you need to check on who I am and what I did, please contact Colonel David E. Opfer of the US Air Force. I worked with Colonel Opfer when he was the American air attaché in Phnom Penh. He can vouch for me. Surely, you can contact Colonel Opfer?"

"Apparently you do not understand the situation at all, Mr. Ouch," the clerk continued in an increasingly superior and emotionless tone of voice. "As a sovereign nation, the country of Thailand has a perfect right to declare which refugees they will accept, as well as how many they will accept and when they will accept them. We here at Camp 007 serve only in an advisory capacity in that area, and we work with the refugees for humanitarian reasons. We—"

"There is absolutely nothing humanitarian about sending innocent people to certain death," SamSan interrupted, appearing even paler than his usual description as being "pale for a Cambodian."

"I understand perfectly how you feel, Mr. Ouch, and I agree with you, but I am not the one who sets the policy. I am simply a clerk working for the United Nations in Camp 007, and I am trying to inform you that the policy of the country of Thailand has recently changed. The country of Thailand is not accepting any further refugees from the country of Cambodia at the present time. I know that does not fit your plan, but that is how it happens to be.

"Our job at Camp 007 is to register your group; give you food and shelter for a reasonable period of time; see that you have supplies for your trip home; and wish you godspeed on that journey. This camp has been intentionally built on the Cambodian side of its border with Thailand," the clerk continued with an air of finality, "so technically, you have never left your country."

SamSan's frown made his bushy eyebrows impinge on his eyes so that their slight oriental slant appeared to be increased. "And that is the final answer, is it? Not any hope for an appeal?"

"Oh yes, we do have a process set up for an appeal. However, I have never seen even one person who has won such an appeal— much less a group of ten."

SamSan forcibly retained his composure. He stood to his full height of five feet six—still a couple or perhaps three inches shorter than the blonde Swedish clerk but taller than most Asian men are. "Where can I file this appeal and how soon can it be filed?"

"I have the forms you will need right here, Mr. Ouch, and you may file your appeal at this time if you wish to do so. Make certain that you press hard enough to make three legible copies. That is very important. Then sign each copy and return all three of them to me."

"Is there a representative from an American Embassy anywhere in the refugee camp?"

"No, Mr. Ouch."

"Do you have any contact with an American embassy? I want to request political asylum in the United States." SamSan's mind raced as he tried to cover all possible solutions to his problem.

"No, Mr. Ouch, no country has an embassy presence here, and I have no contact with any embassy."

"Does anyone from the present Cambodian government see these papers? If Cambodian officials should see them and learn we are still in Cambodia ...? Can you see my problem?"

"Yes, Mr. Ouch, I can definitely see your problem. I assure you that my eyes and those of the Committee on refugees for the country of Thailand are the only eyes that will see these papers. Well, they might possibly be seen by a representative from the United States—if it gets that far."

"Are you a member of that committee on refugees?"

"No, Mr. Ouch, I have nothing to do with that committee."

SamSan gave a slight shrug of his shoulders but held his tongue. Then he was meticulous in filling out the appeal papers that, at the time seemed to be his only hope for a significant future. He appended his signature with a flourish and handed the papers to the receiving clerk. He managed to force a slight bow and a mumbled "Thank you."

Parable of the Small Salmon

As he made his way back to his partners in the escape, SamSan's only fear at that moment was for his own sanity. For some strange reason, all of his fear seemed to vanish suddenly. *Why am I not really worried at a time like this?* he wondered. *And why should my mind be totally consumed by a story I heard as a child in Sunday school? And why do I remember 'The Parable of the Small Salmon' in such great detail?*

It made no sense to him, but in his mind he could clearly hear that parable as Mrs. Allison had told it to him so many years ago:

The small salmon had swum upstream for hundreds of kilometers and had overcome many obstacles along the way. Then she came upon a concrete dam too high for her to jump, even with her great leaping ability. It was impossible for her to swim up its falling waters.

Her long journey had made her very tired, and the small fish felt famished because she had spent many days without food. She was afraid to turn back, because on her upstream journey she had barely escaped the reaching paw of the huge grisly a hundred meters below the dam. She swam about, feeding on smaller fish for several days trying to gain strength. Through it all, she still felt the constant push of her genetic urge to continue her migration and spawn.

Suddenly there flashed in front of her an enticing silver minnow. The small salmon attacked—only to realize too late that she had swallowed a fisherman's lure. Back-and-forth she ran, making a huge jump at the end of each run. While she was airborne in each jump, she shook violently trying to spit out that lure—but nothing happened. Finally, with her last ounce of strength expended, the small salmon gave up her effort to escape and surrendered to the inevitable.

The fisherman, who stood above the dam, gently grasped his prey and removed the painful hooks from the fish's mouth. Immediately, he laid the salmon on his measuring stick. "Drat it," the disappointed angler said, "she is one-half inch too short to keep." He immediately threw the small fish back into the stream. The small salmon realized that she was above the dam and could now continue to follow her genetic urge to spawn.

He even remembered how she had concluded her story: *That is how God sometimes gets us through problems in our lives. His way is sometimes painful but, if we endure, it allows us to reach our goals in life.*

The plight of that mythical salmon did appear quite similar to the predicament SamSan and his group faced at this moment—but why should he remember it now? There was no possible way he could visualize anyone symbolically fishing above this political dam that entrapped his group. Perhaps it was a sign from God that the committee might grant them political asylum as he had requested. *Could that be the reason for my sudden recall of that particular story at a time when much more pressing problems should occupy my mind?* he wondered.

How he wished he could see or in some way get in touch with Colonel Opfer. Surely, that great man could help them get through this morass of political red tape, but there seemed to be no way he could arrange that contact.

A "Family" Consultation

As soon as SamSan reappeared in the holding room, every member of the self-proclaimed "family" excitedly crowded around him. After hours of restless waiting and worrying, they all tried to speak at once:

"What did they say?" "When can we go to America?" "I am hungry." "Where is the bathroom?"

SamSan's downcast demeanor spoke volumes and, even before he could utter a word, the tone of most of their questions and comments changed drastically:

"They are not going to help us. We are as good as dead. I tried to get you not to come," said Keng.

"For God's sake, please do not tell me we are not going to America after all we have been through," Tang muttered.

"When do we get something to eat?" Kang asked.

"I have got to go to the bathroom," said Heav.

"Everybody be quiet," Pong said. "Let SamSan speak."

"The news is not good," SamSan tried hard to stand erect and control the quiver in his voice, "but we must not panic. We will find some way out of here, even if we have to buy or fight our way to freedom. We have come too far to turn back, and I have burned all of my bridges behind me.

"Unfortunately, the receiving clerk has informed me in no uncertain terms that Thailand is no longer accepting any refugees from Cambodia. However, there is an appeal process, and I have already filed an appeal for our entire group," he continued without making mention of the cold water thrown on the appeal process by the reception clerk.

"Hopefully they will find my record or contact my friend Colonel Opfer. Then they might give consideration to my work with the Americans in both Viet Nam and Cambodia. I believe that would clear the way for us."

"Maybe we can bribe a soldier to take us across the border," said Tang. "I have a diamond ring I hid from soldiers in my secret place."

"No, we should not do that yet," said SamSan. "It is too early. We must first play by the rules and not resort to anything illegal or violent. For some reason I have a strange peace about our situation. Maybe it is because of the bright light and the American flag I saw in my dream in Siem Riep; or it could be because of a story my Sunday school teacher taught me as a child. For some reason I remembered that story just now, and I feel in my heart that we will be okay.

"Anyhow, we must not be too hasty. If we do not have an answer in a few days, when we know more about this place and the people who work here, we may need to fall back on bribery—or even violence. Either one is certainly better than death. But for now, it is better if we follow the rules."

"Money, it talks," Tang insisted. "There is always somebody who can be bought with a few coins."

"You are right," said SamSan, "there is always someone who is on the take, but we must try the legal means first. That means we should wait to hear the results of my appeal. In the meantime, each one of us must pray very hard and very often to whatever God he or she believes in. You must ask him to help us out of this mess. At the same time, we must keep our eyes and ears open. Be on the lookout for someone who might have some services for sale that we might use in the future, but do not be too open about it. A thing like that might create more problems than it solves."

SamSan Reflects on His Life

Although he realized that by all appearances their situation was hopeless, SamSan felt no real sense of panic. "How could that be?" he wondered aloud. Yet, ever since he had recalled the short parable about the small salmon, he had felt a strange sense of peace. *Why?*

He had always heard that when a man comes face-to-face with death, his entire life flashes in front of him. Now, vivid pictures began to come to SamSan's mind. He thought of several times when, like now, his future looked somewhere between bleak and hopeless. He especially remembered the stories he had heard about the life-changing dramatic events surrounding his birth and adoption and his encounter in the helicopter with Prak Vannarith; not to mention his out-of-the-blue release from prison by the Khmer Rouge.

In every one of these critical situations, help had always arrived at precisely the right time. Help had always come in a manner that was strange and unexpected, and it was sometimes very painful—exactly as help had come in a strange painful way to the small salmon in the parable. He wondered why he had never made that connection before. Strange.

God Answers Prayer

The very next day, Kang, the adopted son of Pong and Tang, was playing near the fringes of the refugee camp when he suffered a severe injury to his left leg. Speculation was that a Khmer Rouge bamboo booby trap had caused it. Since Camp 007 had no medical care facility at all, SamSan flagged down a passing Red Cross ambulance and informed its Austrian driver about the boy's injury. He asked the driver for transportation to a medical facility for the injured child. The driver seemed hesitant, and SamSan, thinking it would help the child's cause, told the driver about his service to the Americans during the war with Vietnam.

The driver's face turned quite red, and he said rudely, "I do not give a damn about your help to the Americans. My shift is over and I am not taking you or your supposedly injured child anywhere." Then he rolled up the ambulance window and pulled away from a very disappointed and irate Cambodian.

In anger, SamSan thought, *If my service to the Americans means nothing, then I will not tell anyone else about it; and I will not tell them about the languages I speak either. Just let them get along without translators as far as I am concerned.*

He returned to the group and told them of his experience with the ambulance driver and the decision he had made. He went to bed still very angry. However, Kang continued to have pain, and the rest of the group feared a severe infection could set up in his badly bruised and lacerated leg in the unsanitary conditions of the temporary refugee camp. They needed to get treatment for him in a medical facility somewhere.

Tang continued to worry about her son, and her anger at the selfish and self-pitying attitude of the sleeping SamSan became greater and greater. She shook SamSan to wake him from his sleep and demanded, "Get up from there and go back into the camp area, and do not come back until you find some way to get my boy some medical treatment. My son does not need to die just because you are angry and your feelings are hurt."

SamSan relented and headed toward the camp headquarters. He flagged down a different Red Cross ambulance, this one driven by a woman from Denmark whose attitude was entirely different. She listened attentively to his story (though he said nothing about his service to the Americans) and then agreed to carry the entire group into Thailand in her ambulance.

On December 27, 1979, the entire "family" safely enrolled in the Kaoidang Holding Center for Refugees in Thailand. At last there was assurance of safety for their lives and that, in time, their freedom would come. As he stood in amazement at their good fortune and the way it had come about, SamSan mused, *The fisherman standing above the dam has caught and released the small salmon.*

"Lord," he prayed, "I know You are a fisher of men, and I thank You for answering my prayers. However, I simply cannot predict or understand the methods You use in answering those prayers. You continue to amaze me. Amen."

FREEDOM ASSURED
Kaoidang Refugee Holding Center, Thailand—
Late December 1979

Kang's injury panned out not to be as serious as the family had thought at first. The emergency facility at Kaoidang treated his wound and released him to outpatient care. The camp then assigned a small, 20 x 20 meter plot in Section Three of Kaoidang to the family, although they had built no housing in the section at the time, and between three hundred and four hundred people already lived there. To make matters worse, no bathroom facilities existed, and human excrement littered the ground everywhere. The stench of the camp seemed worse to SamSan than that he had endured when he had literally shoveled out the contents of human open-pit toilets during the Pol Pot regime.

And I left a good house the government provided for me and my family to come to this place, he thought. *At least it is not under communist control. Lord, please help me to realize my dream of going to America.*

Late in the afternoon of their first day in the camp, the group received a large supply of rice along with a small amount of dried fish, oil, and salt. They also received a big pile of bamboo and thatches with a packet of directions for constructing their own shelter out of the material. They busied themselves immediately, but night fell before they had made much progress with their structure, and the group had to sleep on the ground contaminated with fecal filth that night. The following day brought enough progress in their building project to allow them at least to sleep on an elevated bamboo floor, and they slept much better.

In spite of the fact that Kaoidang had provided some food and housing for his group, SamSan's anger still seethed against the Austrian ambulance driver. He knew it was unreasonable, but he continued to keep the promise he had made to himself not to let anyone know about his language abilities or his military service. However, the family did not have any milk for David, and the baby began to appear weak and showed early signs of malnourishment. SamSan finally decided it was time for him to put aside his anger and use his language abilities to save his son's life. In desperation, he went directly to the Kaoidang Camp Director's office to seek help.

"I am SamSan Ouch," he said as he met Danny Hill, the assistant camp director and an appointed Southern Baptist missionary from the United States. "My son, David, is too young to eat the food the camp has provided for us, and he is beginning to get very weak. We desperately need some milk for him. Can you help us, please?"

Danny Hill's face became wreathed in smiles as, with Bible in hand, he heard SamSan's desperate plea. As he listened, the eloquence of his visitor's English vocabulary did not escape his notice.

"Of course, we will get some help for your son. I will see to it that he gets a few cases of milk right away," he replied, "and you can count on more when you need it."

Then Hill pressed further. "I do not suppose that you know you may be an answer to our prayers," he said excitedly. "For many months we have been praying and searching for an interpreter with language ability such as yours, and we have not been able to find anyone. Pol Pot apparently killed most of them. How did you survive?"

"Only by the grace of God, sir," SamSan smiled as he answered.

"I love that answer," Danny Hill beamed in reply. "Do you happen to be a Christian?"

When SamSan replied with a "yes," Hill's face brightened even more.

"That is even better," he said. "You will be able to help me with the church services in the camp every Sunday. I can do very well in speaking Thai, but my Khmer is awful."

SamSan Becomes "Somebody"

"In the meantime," Hill continued, "I am going to make you the head of your section beginning right now. That is Section Three, is it not?"

"Yes, it is Section Three, and I will be happy to help you with the church services in any way I can," said SamSan as his smile matched or exceeded that of Danny Hill. "I have truly missed my church for the past four years."

"Do you suppose you can find us some more interpreters?" Hill asked. "We need them desperately to help us with this crowd."

"It is just as you said, Mr. Hill, most of us who speak English were killed by the Khmer Rouge, but I will ask around and see who I can find," SamSan replied as he left the office. His serious search of the camp turned up only four people with a small degree of competence in English.

Reports of his remarkable ability to speak, read, and write both French and English—using correct grammar and exhibiting a large vocabulary—spread rapidly through both the leadership and the rank and file in Kaoidang. He became an instant hit with the camp administration and experienced a meteoric rise in his status. When Danny Hill introduced him to Mark Brown, the United Nations field officer in charge of the entire camp, Mr. Brown asked the young Cambodian to become his personal assistant and to take operational charge of all sections of Kaoidang.

Although they were still deplorable, living conditions in Kaoidang began to improve slowly. However, Thai citizens viewed the camp as a foreign presence in Thailand and a threat to their security, so no one was supposed to leave the camp. Most of the refugees housed there felt almost like prisoners. Those who did slip out often faced arrest and beating by the Thai police, who killed some of them. Others were robbed by Thai citizens who were either unhappy with their presence in Thailand or who realized that these defenseless people were easy marks.

In spite of Thailand's official refusal to accept them, refugees continued to flow into Kaoidang, and soon Area Three became filled to overflowing, as well as Area Four. Only then did the UN provide open-pit public toilets for the entire camp. Even with the public facilities, open sewage continued to trickle through drainage ditches beside the small alleyways of the refugee camp.

Peacemaker

His new assignment required that SamSan work closely with Mr. Brown and Mr. Hill in the daily operation of Kaoidang. They furnished him with a moped to get around the camp, and this became a symbol of his status among the refugees. To SamSan, however, his real status symbol was the key they gave him to the bathroom in the headquarters office. He finally felt he could present himself in public without carrying the stench of the communal pit toilets.

SamSan had hardly begun his new assignment when racial trouble flared between some groups of Chinese and Cambodians. These had happened often before with frequent fights and occasional murders. Acting in his new capacity as the chief section leader, SamSan moved all of the Chinese into section six and helped them form a Chinese refugee association. This racial segregation restored the peace.

The newly established association of Chinese refugees then attempted to elect SamSan as its president, but he declined to serve. Instead, he suggested his friend and benefactor, Chang Ngy, as president. He told the Association about Mr. Chang's experience with his own Chinese Citizens' Committee in Kom Pong K Dey. When Mr. Chang's election occurred with no opposition, SamSan felt he had paid the personal indebtedness he had to his early benefactor.

After SamSan's successful defusing of the explosive situation between Chinese and Cambodians in Kaoidang, Mark Brown came to him and asked, "Are you familiar with the refugee camp called Sakeo?"

"Is that the one where all of the Khmer Rouge refugees are held?" SamSan answered quizzically.

"Yes, and we have quite a dilemma there," said Mark Brown. "You did such a good job in clearing up our problems between the Chinese and the Cambodians here in Kaoidang, I believe you are the man to do this job for us."

"And what is the job you want me to do for you there, Mr. Brown?" SamSan replied, his curiosity aroused.

"The Thai government is very unhappy about having these people inside their borders because of their violent history. There is some logic in that, because a lot of the Khmer Rouge in the camp appear to be trying to reorganize a force so they can go back and join the groups still fighting the Vietnamese. They want to try to retake Cambodia, and they are apparently training some people in Sakeo for that purpose. However, many of the people there seem to have truly changed their mind about the Khmer Rouge and their system of government. They want to relocate in other countries as peaceful citizens," Mark Brown replied.

SamSan showed a trace of a smile as he said, "A long time before the regime fell, I could see evidence that some of the Khmer Rouge cadre were weakening in their support of that way of life. Then there were some who appeared to be really hardcore and felt they were doing the exact best thing for the people of Cambodia. But why are you telling all of this to me?"

"I want you to go to Sakeo and interview every one of the people in the camp. I need them divided into two groups: one group of refugees that have the possibility of becoming refugees in other countries, and one group of them that you feel have no possibility of being integrated into a civilized, democratic society."

"I am not certain I have the capacity to do that," SamSan replied with a grimace, "but I am willing to give it a try. Do you have a form or a list of questions for me to use?"

"No," Mark Brown replied. "You will need to make up that agenda for yourself. You have had enough experience with those people to know how to do that."

"When do I start?" SamSan said, thrilled by the trust the camp administration placed in him.

"Your transportation will be waiting for you when you report for work in the morning," Mark Brown replied. "And I am grateful for your help in this matter."

It took about two weeks for the interviews to be completed. SamSan was surprised at the number of Khmer Rouge who seemed to have experienced a true change of heart and, in his judgment, were capable of rehabilitation. He turned his report over to Mark Brown for referral to higher authorities.

Search for a Son Renewed

As soon he felt securely ensconced in his new leadership role, SamSan familiarized himself with the communication facilities that were available in the UN offices. He asked for and gained permission to use them for personal purposes. Then he began to employ those facilities and all available information to search diligently for any trace of his lost son and brother-in-law in his free time. He also looked for his friends, Colonel Opfer and Jimmy Jacks. When he found them, both of his friends seemed overjoyed that he had survived the almost-impossible four-year ordeal of the Khmer Rouge.

Each of the men felt indebted to the young Cambodian and voluntarily sent him a small gift of money. They also volunteered to make contacts to help in locating his lost son, but neither could find any trace of the boy. On a very positive note, Colonel Opfer gave him a verbal agreement to be the sponsor for SamSan's entire group in the event they should come to America.

By contacting the CMA church headquarters, he was also able to establish contact with Paul Allison and his mother. They too were ecstatic and astonished to hear of his survival and wanted to hear every detail of the incredible ordeals he had endured. However, the Allisons found themselves in no position to consider becoming sponsors of any group of refugees.

When SamSan began the paperwork for his group to finally realize their dream of living in America, Mark Brown and Danny Hill raised strong and selfish objections. They did not want to lose this capable interpreter and proved administrator. When the papers were completed and filed through the proper channels, the countdown to ultimate freedom for SamSan and his protégées had at last begun.

Escorting Royalty and other Dignitaries

In early May of 1980, Mark Brown called SamSan into his office and told him that King Carl XVI and Queen Silva of Sweden had made plans to visit the refugee camp. He wanted his young administrative assistant to become a tour guide again and accompany the royal couple throughout their camp visit. No place and no question would be off limits for the royal guests, and he should explain the complete purpose and operation of the UN-sponsored camp to them.

A few days later, the young interpreter could not hide his great excitement as he climbed into a Land Rover bound for a Thai military airfield in Aranyaprathet. When he met the royal couple and their special guests, the wonderful fragrance of Queen Silva's perfume raised a fear that he might be a carrier of the foul odor that seemed to be an integral part of living in a refugee camp. This fear caused him to keep more distance between himself and the dignitaries than they, or proper protocol, demanded.

The trio boarded a Thai military helicopter along with a two-star general from the Army of Thailand and several members of his staff. At the end of the thirty-minute journey to Kaoidang, SamSan's chest swelled with pride as they circled over the camp and he could see a large group of people gathered to greet them. When they landed in a clearing in the center of Kaoidang, he stepped off the helicopter with that august company to the cheers of the crowd. When Mark Brown the UN Camp Director and a host of other people met them, SamSan felt vindicated from every indignity he had ever suffered. He felt as if he had truly become "somebody."

King Carl and Queen Silva spoke very little English, but with a combination of his English and French, SamSan managed to communicate with them and show them every aspect of refugee camp life that they desired to see. The refugees entertained the royal couple with demonstrations of classical dancing. Many samples of Cambodian art done in Kaoidang, and a host of different handcrafts, skillfully made by the refugees with the crudest of tools, were also on exhibit. They toured the Buddhist temple, the school, and the church. They visited the hospital to witness first hand the many different diseases encountered in the camp. However, the thing that made the royal pair especially happy was to meet their own fellow citizens, Swedish volunteers who served in different capacities in Kaoidang.

Before the royal couple left the camp, the King invited SamSan to immigrate to Sweden and become a citizen there. "Your Majesty," the flattered and smiling guide said, "I am truly overwhelmed by Your Majesty's offer, but since I was a small boy I have had a dream of living in America. I owe so much to my American missionary friends who taught me the language, and I have hopes of seeing them there—as well as my American commanding officer. I am still committed to that dream."

The King gave His Majesty's royal mailing address and telephone number to his tour guide and presented him with a royal mug with His Majesty's picture embossed on it, as well as several other small gifts.

A few weeks later, SamSan would also serve as the tour guide for Malcolm Fraser, the Prime Minister of Australia. He also arranged and guided tours for quite a number of less important figures who visited Kaoidang from time to time.

Nine Thousand Gideon Bibles

Even though the Thai government had closed their border with Cambodia to refugees several months before, refugees continued to pour into Thailand. The government finally placed a considerable number of troops on that border and effectively closed it. This troop concentration caused the Vietnamese government occupying Cambodia to be fearful of an invasion by the Thai army and led to an unstable situation with war-like talk between the two countries. The artillery practice by both armies near the border gave rise to constant rumors of an invasion by the armies on both sides of the border.

The closing of the Thai-Cambodian border created a real dilemma for Danny Hill in the missionary aspect of his life. He had ten thousand Bibles in the Khmer language on hand that the Gideons had supplied to him for distribution to Cambodian refugees. Now that there would be no more refugees, and since he had already saturated the Christian community in the camp with Bible placements, Danny Hill wondered what he could do with those scriptures. He spoke to SamSan about the matter, and they prayed together and asked God to provide a source to get the Bibles into Cambodia.

Simple possession of a Bible had been reason for a death sentence under the Khmer Rouge regime, so the holy books were practically nonexistent in Cambodia at this time. However, the new Vietnamese government had lifted the stringent restrictions on religion, and citizens in that country could now read their Bibles with no fear of death.

One Monday morning shortly after Danny had come into his office, SamSan burst into the room and excitedly said, "Come quickly. I want you to meet a man who is about to leave the refugee camp."

Danny followed SamSan's rapid footsteps as he took him to meet a man who had at one time been an associate pastor of the church SamSan attended in Battambang. Pastor Sonaan had slipped through the border and come into Kaoidang with no intention of becoming a refugee. He had come strictly to get a few Bibles for his church members and was preparing to walk the long distance back over the "killing fields" carrying six or seven of them.

Excited by this apparent answer to his prayer, Danny asked Pastor Sonaan, "Can you meet me at the border? I could bring perhaps a thousand of these Bibles in my Land Rover, and you could meet me with some of your church members and carry them into Cambodia."

"I am certain we could do that," replied Pastor Sonaan. "When would you propose for us to meet?"

"It will probably take two weeks for both of us to get things ready. Can you meet me on Tuesday, the 17th of June?"

"The 17th will be fine."

"And where should we meet?" Danny responded.

"I propose we meet at Machmun, which is exactly on the border between the countries. It is a town that is disputed between Thailand and Cambodia for a long time, so the border is indefinite there, and it is the only place the Thai government does not have total control over border crossings."

"That will be fine. I will meet you in Machmun around ten in the morning of the seventeenth of June."

When he got out of bed on June 17th, Danny Hill already had a thousand Bibles loaded in his Land Rover. Only then did the thought strike him: *I am not supposed to be at the border. In fact, I am supposed not to be there.*

"Lord," he prayed, "if You want me to do this, simply blind their eyes and let me get through. Amen."

Danny drove through checkpoint after military checkpoint only to be waived straight ahead by the Thai military on each occasion. When he reached Machmun, he was amazed at the size of the city. He had expected a small border village, but he encountered a city of about 150,000 people, and he and Pastor Sonaan had made no arrangements of a definite place to meet.

Thinking his trip was in vain, Danny dejectedly got out of his Land Rover and began to try to give out the scriptures. He had given away only six or seven of them when an unknown man appeared and handed him a piece of paper. When Danny looked at the paper, he was surprised to see his own handwriting. Then the realization struck him that God had brought the two parties together within less than ten minutes in this city of 150,000 residents.

Danny made eight more trips to Machmun and delivered 9,000 Gideon Bibles to Pastor Sonaan and the people of Cambodia. On the morning that he was supposed to deliver the last load of scriptures, the Vietnamese overran the city of Machmun. Danny had a premonition of this, so he canceled his last trip and those Bibles went undelivered.

Bound for America

On August 18, 1980, SamSan received word that the United States had accepted his party for relocation there.

When they heard the news, the administrative group at Kaoidang promised him a big promotion with salary adequate to care for his family in America if he would allow Keng and David to go on to their destination, and he could join them later. The tearful SamSan brushed aside their last-minute pleas. Keng's loud cries of, "No, no, do not leave us alone," and the tears running down her cheeks were sufficient argument to turn SamSan against that idea.

The group transferred to Chonburi Transit Center for processing. Each of them underwent a physical examination, urinalysis, multiple blood tests, and chest X-ray. An immigration officer also intensely interviewed every individual in the group. Again, SamSan became an interpreter on a volunteer basis during his short time in the transit center.

After a stay of about six weeks in Chonburi, the group transferred to Rangsit transit center in Bangkok on October 6, 1980. That day, they boarded an airplane bound for Los Angeles with a stopover in Japan. When the group reached Los Angeles, SamSan learned that Colonel Opfer had recently experienced the death of both his mother and father. Because of pressing business affairs, he would be unable to serve as the sponsor for SamSan's group. He also learned that the First Baptist Church of Winder, Georgia, had agreed to accept them immediately.

ADAPTING IS A TWO-WAY STREET
*Winder, Georgia, USA—
October 9, 1980*

As chairman of the church's refugee sponsor committee, I had the pleasure of meeting the tired but happy travelers in the Atlanta airport and welcoming them to the United States. Months of preparation had finally reached their conclusion, and our family had arrived. The group had been in transit from Bangkok, Thailand, for more than sixty hours when they finally arrived in Atlanta.

In short order, the family with their meager baggage boarded the church van bound for their permanent residence in Winder. As we chatted on the way to their new residence, I could not help but consider how God had tested, guided, and blessed our refugee sponsor committee. Whereas the committee had reluctantly agreed to take a family of twelve in which no one spoke English and we had great uncertainty if anyone could work to support the family, that group could not come. On the other hand, this group had six able-bodied adults, and their leader, SamSan, spoke eloquent English—and he was a Christian to boot.

As the church gathered for supper that evening, the new family made every effort to hide the signs of their total exhaustion. In spite of broad smiles and an obvious rush of adrenalin, their tiredness showed. Most of the adults only minced at the food placed in front of them, while the children gulped hungrily. SamSan quickly came to the defense of the adults as he said, "Please do not be offended because we have eaten so little. It is not because we do not like the food. Of course, it is different from our usual fare, but it is very delicious. After so many hours of travel time, we are simply too tired to be truly hungry—and they did give us some food on the airplane. Please accept our apologies."

Every person in the church who had done anything to help get ready for the family really wanted to meet every one of them that night, but unfortunately the major socializing had to wait for another time. They were in dire need of rest, and we still had to help them establish themselves in their new residence.

When the group first viewed their new home, SamSan remarked, "Oh, this is wonderful. There are so many rooms and they are so large—six rooms and a combination kitchen/dinette. We have never had this much space in any home where we have lived before." He began to assign rooms and beds as the family quickly claimed their individual spaces and spread out throughout the house.

The first evidence that we had actually acquired three families instead of one came on a routine check the following morning. They had partitioned off every bedroom in the house with sheets hanging on strings to provide privacy and separation for the families and for different sexes within each family. In spite of this unexpected use of the bed sheets, we found that the generosity of the congregation had resulted in an adequate number to cover every bed.

The routine check the following morning also showed that the bacon and eggs we had supplied for them did not emit the same aroma as when most Southern kitchens cook them. The smell made it obvious that our family had brought a supply of Oriental spices with them. Only then did we realize we had given no thought to a source of supply for foods of their ethnic choosing and that we needed to locate an adequate Oriental food store in the near future.

In most respects, however, our planning had been on target, and a healthy relationship quickly developed between the refugee family and a great majority of our church family and the community at large. Each side seemed to want to cater to the needs of the other. The major problem that we faced—the language barrier—could only be settled by time and patience.

Small-Town Gossip

The small town of Winder had not seen as much excitement since the McDidit murder trial that resulted in two mistrials before the jury eventually accepted the defense claim that the dog had shot and killed Mr. Mac's wife. The gossip reached a peak shortly after the ten Cambodian refugees arrived in town. Bridge clubs and business conferences, garden clubs and golf carts, private conversations and public communication lines reverberated with small talk and pure gossip about every aspect of the story. In my crowded waiting room, I overheard several snatches of anonymous conversation among my patients that demonstrated empathy with our new family:

"You have got to feel sorry for those poor people. I cannot picture myself having to go to some foreign land carrying everything I owned on my back as they have had to do. They must start their lives over—completely from scratch."

"That would be tough. But can you imagine moving to a place where you cannot even read a street sign or look up a number in a telephone book?"

"Yeah, and you cannot ask directions because nobody can understand what you say, and you could not understand them even if they gave you an answer. It has to be tough."

"They act very nice, but all they seem to be able to do is bow and smile. I am sure glad I am not the one that has responsibility for them. Doc has a tough job on his hands."

DR. C B SKELTON

On the other hand, my barber reported a number of detractors who predicted dire consequences from this "invasion of foreigners."

"No good can come from that bunch of heathens coming here. This country is already full of riff-raff, and that is why our taxes are so high. Doc did not do us any favor by bringing people like that to America. They will wind up taking jobs that real Americans ought to have."

"No telling what kind of disease they might have brought with them. I hear about all kinds of TB and malaria and even leprosy over there where they come from. We spent a whole lot of years getting this country rid of that kind of stuff, and I surely do not want us to have to go through that again."

"Better keep your eye on your dogs and cats. They tell me they are delicacies to folks like them."

Fortunately, a host of people rushed to lend a hand in providing whatever needs the new arrivals might have. Volunteers enrolled their children in local schools; taught English as a second language and driving American style; secured employment for the adults; assisted with local shopping; and opted for a wide variety of other tasks.

SamSan could speak seven languages (counting four dialects of Chinese as only one language). He spoke English with a moderate accent, but he had a very large vocabulary and used almost-perfect grammar. That provided a great deal of comfort to our volunteers, but it did not eradicate the language barrier. Eight other people in the group needed some type of individual instruction, with only the infant, David, excepted. This led to some harried, and some humorous, incidents to spice up the local gossip.

A Special Occasion

On the first Sunday after the new family's move to Winder, every person in the congregation of the First Baptist Church sat on the edge of his or her seat waiting for them to enter the sanctuary. No one seemed to be admiring the deep color tones of the Tiffany stained-glass window that depicts Jesus as having six toes and carrying a lamb in His arms. No child appeared to be counting the one hundred forty-four bulbs in the beautiful chandeliers overhead. The haunting strains of Beethoven's *Ode to Joy* came from the hallowed Schantz pipe organ only to fall on muted ears. When, at the last minute, the family marched into the church in single file and filled the second row on the left front side of the church, a hush fell over the congregation.

One could tell at first glance that the volunteer ladies had done well in advising the Asian women about choices in clothing. Each of the refugee females had made a beautiful selection from the racks of donated dresses and pantsuits that hung in their new home. They looked wonderful in their western-style garb, and several women in the audience showed great delight on seeing one of their former favorite outfits given a second chance.

However, it became just as obvious that someone had fallen short in explaining about the styles in western world accessories. Each of the women carried her Cambodian language Bible and a spotlessly clean, beautifully folded, fluffy washcloth. The titter that went throughout the church was subdued, and yet it was obvious.

When church dismissed, I said to SamSan, "Your ladies did a beautiful job in choosing their clothing and in washing and folding those pieces they carried in their hands this morning. I never thought washcloths could be so beautiful."

He smiled broadly and bowed as I continued. "But those are not formal handkerchiefs they were carrying in their hands. They are called 'washcloths,' and washcloths are designed to be used with soap and water to scrub your hands at a sink or your body in a bathtub."

SamSan suppressed a sheepish grin as he explained, "We had never seen anything like them before, and we tried and tried to figure what to do with them. Finally, somebody said they looked like the grand kerchiefs that fine ladies in Cambodia carry on special occasions—and this certainly ranked as a special occasion to us."

"And to us also," I responded as I blinked back my tears.

American Fast-Food

A few days after our family's arrival in Winder, Donnie and Nancy, owners of the local Dairy Delite and members of the First Baptist Church, hosted the group's first exposure to American fast-food. From the moment I steered the church van away from their home until it came to a halt in the Dairy Delite's parking lot, a constant, excited chatter came from the group. The chatter stopped abruptly as they scrambled off the bus and marched into the food establishment, where a few interested church members had gathered.

None of the family had any idea about what to order. SamSan had tried to explain to them about hamburgers and hot dogs, but he had never seen or tasted one of the truly American creations. Donnie and Nancy gave each family member a hot dog complete with coleslaw and pickles, a hamburger "all the way," French fries, and a large Coca-Cola.

Most of the newcomers showed vague familiarity with Coca-Cola but commented that it had been years since they had tasted any type of soft drink. However, the hamburgers and hot dogs were a new experience for every one of our charges. Tiny nibbles and quizzical looks seemed to be the rule among the adults as I watched them intently and rubbed mustard from my own chin.

Every one of the church members present had a special interest in a specific refugee because they had volunteered to guide and assist that person in some particular aspect of his or her life. "How do you like American fast-food?" became the most common question of the hour.

"I like," said one.

"Good," said another.

"I am not familiar with those particular spices," SamSan answered in honesty.

Either the children liked the food or they did not like it. Their answers showed clearly in their ketchup smudged or un-smudged faces.

Employment

No matter how well qualified the individual might appear to be or what jobs they had held in Cambodia, the jobs secured for each of our refugees were at basic starting levels and brought them only minimum wage salaries. The committee wanted them to earn their way up in the community.

SamSan and Samsien signed on at the Winder rug mill; Tang toiled at the local plant manufacturing waistbands for pants; Lan labored as an operator in a sewing plant; while Pong proudly produced at the hardest assignment of them all—in a concrete block manufacturing facility. Every one of the newcomers accepted his or her assignment without complaint and quickly drew rave reviews from their employers for their diligence and excellent work.

A false rumor spread wildly throughout the community, saying, "Foreign people like them do not pay any taxes. That's why our taxes are so high."

"That is a blatant lie," I said to each person who reported that rumor to me. "Their very first paychecks had taxes taken from them on exactly the same scale as any other paycheck in Georgia. Furthermore, our plan of education for them does not include any information about the welfare system. We will not encourage them to apply for any type of support or any government grants. They will soon support themselves completely and will contribute to our economic system rather than taking from it. And, furthermore, you can tell your false rumor spreader that the church has done everything we have done without a single dime of state or federal assistance."

Although not one of them applied for any type of government assistance, it did not take our new family long to learn every small bit of information about the welfare system in Georgia. To me it seemed highly ironic that most of their knowledge about public assistance came from the same people who had complained the loudest about their presence in this country.

Strange New Things

A number of things among the donated items stored in the refugee residence and turned over to them without any explanation panned out to be items they had never seen in their native land. Trying to decipher the purpose of each item often taxed the imaginations of the entire group. The item in question on one particular occasion was a simple three-piece, chenille bathroom set. Nevertheless, to our new Cambodian family, it was an enigma—a puzzle. "What is it?" asked SamSan.

"I do not know for sure," said Tang as she put the commode lid cover on her head and cavorted around the room, "but I think this is some type of a hat."

When the others roared in laughter, she curtsied and said, "See, you can make it fit any head size by pulling the strings tight and tying them."

"You may be right, but it does not fit you too well or make you look pretty," said Lan as she laughed and picked up the piece with the rounded cutout designed to fit around the base of the commode. "I believe this is some kind of a bib," she commented as she pulled the piece up close with its "legs" around her neck.

"But how do you keep it on?" asked Keng with an uncharacteristic burst of laughter. "There are no strings for you to tie it on with."

"Do you suppose the latex on its back is designed to make it cling to your clothes and hold it in place?" SamSan asked with a chuckle.

"That is possible," said Lan, "but it sure is heavy and it would be mighty hot."

By this time, the entire family had joined in the festivities as each one tried to figure a purpose for each part of the three-piece set. It had become one of the rare times of pure family fun.

Picking up the matching area throw rug from the set, SamSan sat down in a rocking chair and covered the lower part of his body with it. "This must be a lap robe," he said as he rocked back and forth, "but again, it is very heavy, and it has that sticky stuff on the back of it."

Still quite puzzled but having had a brief respite from the many cares of the world, the group decided they would ask "Miss Carolyn" the next morning. When Carolyn showed them the function for each piece of the set, they merely shook their heads and smiled. The fear of losing face kept them from daring to share with her the details of their puzzlement the night before. More than five years later, SamSan's body shook with laughter as he shared with me the details of that joyous evening together.

Driver's Education

Despite having many years of experience and being a certified teacher of driver education, Ray faced his task of teaching Tang to drive with great trepidation. He looked at all the negatives, the largest being the huge language barrier. When you added the fact that he would be teaching an adult, over whom his position as assistant school principal gave him no authority, and that he would be using his own automobile without an alternate set of controls, he had cause for his angst. Nevertheless, he had promised to do this, and he had to keep his promises. Ray's silent prayer to God for protection rose even more ardently than usual as he took his place in the right front seat of his automobile.

His instructions from other church members who had become volunteer teachers had been, "Keep your sentences simple—only two or three words—usually a subject, a verb, and a predicate. Remember, she has as much difficulty understanding your speech as you have in understanding hers. She does not have the experience in accepting instructions that you have in teaching, and this is her first lesson."

As Tang took her place under the steering wheel, Ray began his instructions with, "You start engine."

Tang turned the ignition key, and the car engine purred to life. "You shift gears. Set to drive," said Ray as he pointed to the gearshift lever and the "D" on the steering wheel column. Tang complied.

"You press accelerator," Ray continued as he pointed to the foot-feed before grabbing the handgrip above his door when the car suddenly lurched from the curb. "You slow down!" Ray shouted as he regained his equilibrium.

"You stop here," he warned as they approached the first stop sign. "Do not be afraid." He tried to be reassuring on seeing a frightened look on Tang's face that nearly matched the fear he could feel etched on his own.

Ray tried to sound calm as he said, "You turn left."

"You *slow down!*" Ray virtually screamed as the car jerked violently to the left and he thought he felt the wheels on one side leave the ground. "Do not be afraid," he repeated as he unconsciously smoothed the hair he could feel standing straight up on his head and silently thought, *I am already frightened enough for both of us.*

The driving lesson continued with a constant flow of two or three-word commands, "You turn right. You slow down. You stop. You slow down. You turn left. You slow down. You signal. You slow down. You..." for about an hour before the car finally came to a well-controlled stop in front of the old house.

"You did well," Ray complimented the broadly smiling Tang as he walked unsteadily around the car to return to his home.

He drove a couple of blocks to his bank's drive-in window and said as he placed his paycheck in the teller drawer, "You cash check?"

Education

The local school system had no way to prepare in advance for the advent of the three Cambodian children. The situation was far different from the one they had faced when the large number of Spanish-speaking students came into the system a few years before. They had teachers of Spanish already in the system, but no one in the local system spoke Khmer, and no one who spoke the language seemed to be available in this area of Georgia except SamSan, who was always at work.

Frustrated teachers and school administrators were creative in their efforts to provide a learning atmosphere for the new students. Nevertheless, those efforts met with only limited success, in spite of their great desire to provide these students with an adequate education. When they reached out to the Georgia State Department of Education for help, the results were disappointing. Other school systems in Georgia that served Eastern Asian immigrants also faced similar problems, and none of them had sufficient assets to deal with the situation.

It had been more than five years since Heav and Ren had received any type of schooling (with the exception of a few lessons in the makeshift classroom at Kaoidang). In addition, they had been on near-starvation diets for an extended period at a critical time in their development; therefore, these girls had great difficulty in learning to read. Now the system expected them to perform in a classroom taught in a language they had little experience with—a language they could neither read, nor write, nor clearly understand. Through the diligent efforts of their teachers and a few church volunteers, they soon began to speak a few words of English; but to comprehend the meaning of those strange words when they tried to read them from the printed page proved virtually impossible for them.

Neither of the girls ever evidenced anything but the best attitude about their schoolwork. However, these obstacles made it impossible for them to meet the educational requirements of the system. The school placed them at about a third-grade level, much lower than their chronological age would have called for under normal conditions. The girls made every effort to learn, but the language barrier was simply too great for them to overcome quickly. As soon as they were old enough to withdraw from school legally, both of them dropped out and entered the work force.

On the other hand, Kang, only ten and quite intelligent, picked up the spoken and written language quickly. He began to function in school near his expected grade level.

THE SEARCH
FINALLY ENDS

Our church-sponsored family had been in Winder for nearly three years. Pong and Tang had purchased their own home and moved out of the old house. Lan, Samsien, and Heav had quickly followed suit. This left only SamSan and Keng in the original residence with their children, David and Samuel. Keng was pregnant with her fourth child (her second in America). She still stayed at home to care for the children and keep house. SamSan still worked his regular shifts at the rug mill, which appeared to be on its way to closing because of the beginning textile crisis. He had the promise of a job at the local Johns-Manville plant, but it had not materialized at the time.

SamSan busied himself in his off time searching every avenue for his lost son, Huot. He wrote to both of the senators from Georgia asking for help in locating the boy, and he contacted every refugee camp in Thailand to see if his brother-in-law, Nai Muoy, had passed through with a child, possibly named Huot. He contacted Danny Hill, Mark Brown, and Buzz Thompson to request a search of every record in the UN's database for evidence of the pair. Colonel Opfer and Captain Jimmy Jacks tried to use their own contacts to locate Huot, but it all appeared to be to no avail.

By now, the boy would be about eight years old, and SamSan felt he could not afford to continue to spend as much time and money as he had been spending on his search for his lost son. By this time, his third son had been born, and he reminded himself that he had a great responsibility to them. His family deserved more attention than he had given them. The time had come to give up hope for his lost son. Sadly, he had to admit to himself finally that Huot had not survived.

A few weeks after SamSan made that decision, a letter came addressed to Ouch SamSan in care of the Pastor, First Baptist Church, Winder, Georgia, USA. It bore a postmark from Paris, France. The pastor delivered it immediately to SamSan, who recognized it as being from a family friend and former next-door neighbor, Sok Houng, who had become a refugee in France. With trembling hands, he opened the letter and read:

> Dear SamSan,
> I am happy to bring you good news. Yesterday, I spoke to a friend of mine here in Paris who recently visited some friends and kinfolk in Phnom Penh. They were talking about what had happened to many mutual friends, and the question came up about your family. She seemed to know all about the deaths of your mother and father and about all the things that had happened to your wife and your brother.
> The good news is that her friend told her that your son, Huot, is still alive and back in Battambang. She said that your brother-in-law, Nai Mouy, returned to his home with the boy shortly after you left Cambodia. For many months, they managed somehow to hide out and avoid the Khmer Rouge. Perhaps the Americans will allow you to bring your son there to live with you, if the boy wishes to come.
> As soon as I heard the news, I started a search to find out how I might contact you. I finally succeeded in contacting a Mr. Danny Hill at Kaoidang, and he told me that the First Baptist Church in Winder, Georgia, USA, had sponsored your group, and he gave me this address.
> I hope you get this letter and I wish you and Huot good luck.
> Kindest regards from your friend,
> Sok Houng

SamSan could hardly believe what he was reading. His son was alive after all these years. However, she had not given him an address for the boy. How could he contact Huot? He had to call Paris and speak with Sok Houng right away.

When he finally reached his friend by telephone, SamSan's voice trembled with excitement. "Sok Houng," he said, "you said in your letter that you have heard my son, Huot, is still alive."

"Yes, SamSan, that is what my friend told me," she replied.

"Oh, that is such wonderful news, but you did not tell me how to get in touch with him. I can hardly wait to talk to him. Can you tell me how I can send him a letter or call him on the telephone?"

"I am sorry, SamSan," she replied, "but the person who told me about him had heard it from someone in Phnom Penh, who had heard it from someone else in Battambang or somewhere. All I know is that she said he is back in Battambang and that he is healthy and growing, but I do not have an address. I am not even certain if they are living in the same house as before, but even if they were, the address would have changed under the new communist government.

"I will contact my friend here in Paris and get the address of her friend in Phnom Penh. Then I will mail that to you right away. Perhaps you can get an address, or you might even get a telephone number from her where you can contact Mouy and Huot. I hope you get in touch with them soon."

The two weeks it took for his letter to arrive from Sok Houng in Paris seemed like an eternity to SamSan. He was ecstatic to have the information on how to contact the person who might help him contact his son. In the meantime, he got in touch with his old friends from Cambodia, Jimmy Jacks and Colonel Opfer, requesting a loan to finance his search for Huot. Both of them sent outright gifts immediately to help their friend to whom they owed so much.

With the address finally in hand, SamSan wrote to Sok Houng's friend's friend in Phnom Penh. He explained his dilemma and requested an address and/or telephone number for Nai Mouy in

Battambang so he could contact his son, Huot. Again, the seemingly interminable wait lasted two and a half months before he received Mouy's mailing address and could pen a letter to him.

That letter revealed that Mouy and Huot were not in Battambang as Sok Houng had told him. They had moved to Phnom Penh, where they lived with Mouy's mother-in-law. SamSan immediately sat down and wrote to his son and brother-in-law:

Dear Huot and Nai Mouy,

You cannot imagine how happy I am to hear the two of you are alive. When I looked for you in Battambang, a neighbor told me that you had tried to get out of Cambodia and had disappeared completely. The person to whom I spoke told me about Guek's death, and he presumed the two of you were dead also.

Huot, I have prayed for you constantly since you were almost four years old and I first learned about your birth. You might never understand all of the circumstances, but my failure to be a father to you was not of my own choosing. I had no idea that your mother was pregnant when the Cambodian military arrested me. We had been trying to have a baby for six years without success.

When I came out of prison, the Khmer Rouge would not allow me to come to Battambang to look for your mother. Had they allowed me to do this, I would have been right by your side throughout your lifetime. I am very sorry to have failed you up until this time, but I would love very much to be a father to you from this time on.

I am now living in America and am very happy here. I hope you will want to come and live with me. My three other sons, David, Samuel, and John, are excited about having an older brother and want to show you how life is here in America. Now that I know you are alive and I have your address, I am already beginning the process of trying to sponsor you to come to America as a refugee. Please let me know if

you would be willing to come here in the event I am successful in getting permission to sponsor you.

Mouy, I shall always be grateful to you for looking after
my son when I could not. I hope there will be some way I can
repay you some day. I am not a rich man, but perhaps you may
have some small needs where I can be of some help to you.
Please let me know about this when you answer this letter. If
there is a telephone where I might reach you, please send me
the number and instructions as to how I could call you.

Gratefully,
Your Father and brother-in-law,
SamSan

SamSan waited impatiently for another two and one-half months
before he received an answer to his letter. When the letter arrived, he
ripped the envelope open and hungrily devoured its contents with a
mixture of emotions as he read:

Dear SamSan,

We were happy to get your letter and to know that you are
alive and well in America. Just as you had heard and feared
that we were dead, we had heard the same things about you.
Huot was glad to know that he has a "real live" father, but he
finds it hard to make up his mind to leave me, the only father
he has known for his entire lifetime, and go to live with a
person he has never met. I suppose that is reasonable for a
person as young as he is.

The telephone service here is very bad and very expensive.
We do not have a telephone in our home, but there is a telephone booth nearby. You can call me person-to-person and
have someone come and get me, or you could call station-to-
station and hope that whoever answers could find me quickly
so the bill would not be so very high. I have written the phone
number at the bottom of this letter.

Huot and I are healthy, and he is growing into a fine
young man. He is studying English in school, because my

wife and I told him how much the English language meant to you. I am sending you a picture of him so you can know what your son looks like right now.

My mother-in-law and my wife send you their greetings and they want you to know how happy they are that you have survived the horrible ordeal under Pol Pot. They would also like to come to America, but I know you cannot bring everyone there.

I am anxious to hear from you again. Please write or call very soon and send us a picture of you and your family. Huot says he would love to hear your voice and to see what you and his brothers look like.

Your brother-in-law,
Nai Mouy

SamSan could hardly wait to place a person-to-person telephone call to Huot in Cambodia, but he found that a call of just five minutes cost about $50. He knew he could not afford to call very often on his near-minimum-wage salary. It excited SamSan to hear the few stumbling English words that his son could speak, and he encouraged him to continue his study of the English language. In his conversation, he confirmed that Huot might be willing to consider coming to America but was loathe to leave the only father he had ever known. He also verified that Mouy had no interest in making such a dramatic life change.

Over the next few years, SamSan called his son whenever he felt he could afford it, but he made virtually no progress in getting Huot to make a firm commitment to come to America. In 1989, he decided to make one last effort for a physical reunion with his son. He had saved up his vacation time from the Johns-Manville plant, and he took a trip to Thailand in hopes of making a personal visit to Huot.

When he arrived in Thailand, he stayed with his half-sister and enjoyed a time of reunion with his Thai family. He was saddened to learn that his mother had died, but his half-brothers treated him royally and gave a huge party in his honor. They helped him scout out the situation in Cambodia and to make the decision that SamSan should not personally go into that country, because he would still be a wanted person there. The risk of his arrest by Cambodian authorities on charges of deserting his post remained too great. If that should happen, he could not return to America, and his son in Cambodia would not be the only one deprived of a father.

SamSan decided he could not afford to take that risk. Instead, he and his half-brothers hired a scouting party to go into Cambodia and speak to Huot and Mouy. They hoped that these personal representatives might be able to bring the boy to Aranyaprathet near the Cambodian border for a vacation. Perhaps if he could become personally acquainted with his father, Huot might change his mind. Huot had other plans at the time and refused to leave his father and come with SamSan's emissaries, even for a vacation. However, it did impress him that his father would go to such lengths to try to meet him.

Even though SamSan considered this trip a failure, it apparently brought a change of heart to Huot. From that time on, he spoke more favorably to his family about coming to America. About a year later, he made the decision to allow SamSan to submit the application to sponsor him as a refugee.

SamSan immediately applied to the US government to be a sponsor for his son to come to America. He had seen many of his friends use illegal means to bring family members here, but SamSan determined he would do things the right way, even though the process seemed extremely slow and painful. After six years of intense negotiation, the word finally came down that the US State Department had accepted Huot to come as a refugee and join his family in Georgia. By this time, SmSan had purchased his own home and could provide adequate lodging for his son.

He could also provide employment for Huot because, from his first day at Johns-Manville, he had worked as much overtime as the company would allow, and had been conservative with his money.

Dr. C B Skelton

He had become the proud proprietor of the Hong Kong Restaurant, a brand-new, modern restaurant in Winder that served Chinese cuisine. Keng managed the restaurant with the capable assistance of their three sons, David, Samuel, and John.

I was privileged to witness a touching reunion in the Atlanta International Airport in mid-June of 1997, as SamSan first laid his eyes on his son, now nearly twenty-two years old. The unbelievable saga of the lost son had finally come to a happy conclusion.

Epilogue

SamSan was overjoyed to have all four of his sons together with him in America at last. The time he had dreamed of and had prepared for over many years had finally come.

SamSan gave Huot immediate employment, and he began training as a cook in the now well-established restaurant. He showed quite an aptitude for this type of work and brought with him a number of ideas from his native land that improved the operation and the menu of the Hong Kong Restaurant.

SamSan continued to work for Johns-Manville to provide insurance for his family, but he no longer worked the long overtime hours, preferring to spend every possible hour working with his family in their new restaurant.

He is now completely retired from public employment and spends all of his time with his family and his restaurant.

SamSan is completely deaf. Increasing scarring of the delicate structures of both of his ears from the severe concussion he received in his near-fatal accident in Kom Pot City has totally ablated his hearing over the years, despite repeated surgeries and numerous hearing aids. The culture in which he was reared makes him lose face when he admits to any flaw, so he smiles and bows as if he understands everything. He can read lips on some individuals.

My communication with him is through writing questions or comments. Then, I prepare myself for the flood of words that follow and give indication of the loneliness his lack of hearing has imposed on him.

SamSan's love for the United States is still unfailing, and his love for his family is ever increasing. He invites all of his friends to visit him at the Hong Kong Restaurant in Winder, Georgia, where he has truly become *a simple seller of noodles*.